GEOFFREY CAINE
RENATE N. CAINE

Strengthening and Enriching Your
Professional
Learning
Community

THE ART OF LEARNING TOGETHER

ASCD
Alexandria, Virginia USA

1703 N. Beauregard St. • Alexandria, VA 22311-1714 USA
Phone: 800-933-2723 or 703-578-9600 • Fax: 703-575-5400
Website: www.ascd.org • E-mail: member@ascd.org
Author guidelines: www.ascd.org/write

Gene R. Carter, *Executive Director;* Judy Zimny, *Chief Program Development Officer,* Nancy Modrak, *Publisher;* Scott Willis, *Director, Book Acquisitions & Development;* Carolyn Pool, *Acquisitions Editor;* Julie Houtz, *Director, Book Editing & Production;* Darcie Russell, *Editor;* Georgia Park, *Senior Graphic Designer;* Mike Kalyan, *Production Manager;* Valerie Sprague, *Typesetter;* Carmen Yuhas, *Production Specialist*

Process Learning Circles[SM] is a service mark of Geoffrey Caine and Renate N. Caine.

All web links in this book are correct as of the publication date below but may have become inactive or otherwise modified since that time. If you notice a deactivated or changed link, please e-mail books@ascd.org with the words "Link Update" in the subject line. In your message, please specify the web link, the book title, and the page number on which the link appears.

PAPERBACK ISBN: 978-1-4166-1089-2   ASCD product #110085   n11/10

Also available as an e-book (see Books in Print for the ISBNs).

Quantity discounts for the paperback edition only: 10–49 copies, 10%; 50+ copies, 15%; for 1,000 or more copies, call 800-933-2723, ext. 5634, or 703-575-5634. For desk copies: member@ascd.org.

Library of Congress Cataloging-in-Publication Data
Caine, Geoffrey.
    Strengthening and enriching your professional learning community : the art of learning together / Geoffrey Caine and Renate N. Caine.
        p. cm.
    Includes bibliographical references and index.
    ISBN 978-1-4166-1089-2 (pbk. : alk. paper)   1. Professional learning communities.
I. Caine, Renate Nummela. II. Title.
    LB1731.C217 2010
    370.71'55—dc22
                                                                                                              2010029134

20 19   18 17 16 15 14 13 12 11 10   1 2 3 4 5 6 7 8 9 10 11 12

To Francisco,
without whose teaching this
book could not have been written

Strengthening and Enriching
Your Professional Learning Community
The Art of Learning Together

Acknowledgments

We have had the pleasure of working with some wonderful people in the many years that it has taken to develop the process described in this book. First and foremost is our friend and colleague Carol McClintic, whose constant support and passion are truly remarkable. Sam Crowell, coauthor with us of *Mindshifts* (1999), was with us in the very early years as we developed this process. Others who have contributed more than we can properly thank them for are Andrea Bond, Lance Fogle, Adam Gratt, and Michael Voell. Special thanks are due to Carolyn Pool, our extremely insightful and patient editor, who was midwife to our first book, *Making Connections: Teaching and the Human Brain*, as well as to this one; and to Darcie Russell, our project manager, for her wonderful patience, clarity, and support. Thanks also to Rosanna Gallagher for reading the manuscript, as well as for being a great educational leader.

Introduction

One of the most underused resources available to educators is the community of colleagues with whom they work. Such communities are invaluable when they work well because a great way to learn and develop as a professional is to do so in partnership with others who are doing the same thing.

The importance of educators learning together is now so clear that the February 2009 issue of *Educational Leadership* was devoted to ways in which collective learning can take place. For instance, Ruth Chung Wei, Alethea Andree, and Linda Darling-Hammond, in their article "How Nations Invest in Teachers," consider several countries that score high on international measures and report that professional development programs in those nations provide time for learning and collaboration, offer job-embedded professional development, and encourage teacher participation in decision making. And, in their article "Teacher Learning: What Matters?" Darling-Hammond and Nikole Richardson argue that teacher professional development should be a sustained effort, should be integrated with school improvement, and should include professional learning communities. A similar philosophy has emerged in the corporate and nonprofit worlds, where one of the most powerful forms of professional development is a "community of practice" (Lave & Wenger, 1991).

In education, working together in this way extends beyond learning to dealing with practical issues that affect us collectively and individually, such as determining how best to use resources or clarifying the path that a school should take. It really helps to work things through with colleagues, both formally and informally.

Understanding Community

Although increasing attention is being paid to the importance of learning communities in schools and elsewhere, much of what is done misses the point because of a failure to recognize that every effective community depends on creating the right underlying conditions. We describe this as *putting community in community*. At a minimum, an overall atmosphere of "relaxed alertness" is essential (see Chapter 1 for more on this topic). As we have written elsewhere, relaxed alertness consists of a general climate and personal states of mind that combine low threat with high intrinsic challenge (Caine, G., & Caine, R., 2001; Caine, R., Caine, G., McClintic, & Klimek, 2008).

Creating these conditions is more important than ever. Nowadays almost every educator feels strong pressure to produce results—an expectation that has been framed largely in terms of raising test scores. Pressure has come from every segment of the community, including parents, politicians, the media, business, philanthropic foundations, and academia. Pressure comes from other sources as well, including overcrowded classrooms, the need to implement mandated programs, and a host of community-related issues. Thus ABC News online reported in 2007 that

> *Inner city high school teachers* [emphasis added], police officers, miners and air traffic controllers are among those with the most stressful jobs in America, according to *Health* magazine. (http://abcnews.go.com/GMA/WomensHealth/story?id=3726457&page=1)

Yet another problem is that the pace of society itself is accelerating to keep up with the speed of technology. At some point the constant rushing becomes both unhealthy and unproductive.

Strengthening and Enriching Your

Professional
Learning
Community

SUSTAINABLE
FORESTRY
INITIATIVE

Certified Fiber Sourcing
www.sfiprogram.org

The net result is that most educators are experiencing a great deal of stress. This book is not the place to talk generally about stress and work. However, it is the place to point out a powerful, paradoxical, and self-defeating aspect to the almost universal sense of urgency about raising standards. To put it bluntly, too much stress makes everyone less effective. All of us. No one is immune. But in environments immersed in excessive stress, neither educators nor students can function optimally. As a result, the system is handicapped in its efforts to raise standards.

The issue, for the purposes of this book, is that by building an effective and healthy learning community, a school can substantially reduce the stress felt by those who work and learn within it, and they can therefore function more effectively—and get better results. In any community, a key factor is relationships and how they are formed. Some ways of being together facilitate a process, but others impede it. People need to listen to and respect each other, even though they may have major differences of opinion and varying goals. They need to feel safe in a group to express and test opinions and to agree and disagree. And they need to respect the overall process and be able to handle issues that persist over time and that vary in degree of difficulty. All this means that any effective and sustainable learning community needs to have some accepted protocols for talking and behaving, and an atmosphere conducive to effective functioning.

We provide guidelines in this book for creating those conditions by means of what we call "process learning circles," or PrLC. We have been developing, testing, and refining the concept for more than 15 years, and have researched and written in depth about our first major five-year projects (Caine, R. & Caine, G., 1997a), as well as about the use of the process in a single-year program of professional development (Caine, R., 2008).

Our process is moderately structured to ensure that all the necessary phases are present and mastered. However, individual aspects of the process can become the foundation for different sets of skills to be employed in different circumstances, as the need arises.

Why "Process"?

Life is a process. We are a process. The universe is a process.

—*Anne Wilson Schaef, author and lecturer*

Creating an instant learning community does not involve following a "recipe." No such recipe exists. All communities and individuals, like all relationships, are works in progress. So we use the word *process* to convey the notion that the development of a great community is an ongoing undertaking. We all have to constantly deal with glitches, allow for some people to move into the community and others to move out, adapt to people's different perspectives of a situation, and more. The goal is to develop and then sustain a climate and a culture that help to make work a pleasure and provide new understandings that are ongoing and that make it possible for people to face challenges together.

All the various phases of the process learning circles, which are covered in detail in the following chapters, develop skills—"process muscles"—to aid in this endeavor. We look at listening, questioning, personalizing ideas, taking action and reflecting on that action, becoming more aware of how we function as individuals with varied learning and decision-making styles, and more. Over time, a "field of listening" is created so that the school's general culture and climate emphasize listening and dialogue, with the field spilling over into individual classrooms, the front office, and other places where people meet and work.

Professional Development

The goal of process learning circles is professional development that works. It is all well and good to attend conferences and workshops and to talk and think about ideas, but it is another thing altogether to be able to use those ideas appropriately in the field and in the classroom. Appropriate use is real-world competence, which includes but goes beyond intellectual understanding.

There is no secret to learning for real-world performance. It always requires a combination of theory and practice, concepts and experience, understanding and action. On the one hand, any program to be mastered involves specified content—ranging from subject-matter mastery to instructional design to habits of mind. On the other hand, the content of any program needs to be personalized and internalized. It has to be *real* to the participants, and that means that it must be personally experienced in a sufficiently rich and individual way. For instance, while teachers explore ways to help students learn together, it is useful to reflect on all the ways in which they, the teachers, have learned with others—both formally and through informal conversations.

So *process* also means "learning from experience" as individuals come to see and to act in new ways. Sustained improvement calls for new content and skills to be experienced. Action, trial and error, experimentation, and feedback on action are essential. But experience alone is not enough. Experience needs to be digested—or processed. Participants need to think about, reflect on, and generally examine what happens in the course of introducing new programs to fully benefit from and make sense of them.

Yet today's schools all too often overlook the aspect of learning from experience, for both students and educators. To successfully change behavior and attitudes, people have to make sense of things at a deep level—to get ideas and procedures "in their feelings" or in their bodies—so that those ideas and procedures are personalized to the point that they can be used naturally and appropriately in the real world of the school, the classroom, and beyond. In our work, we have called this "active processing" (see Chapter 1). It is an essential ingredient in reflective practice.

So our approach to professional development is openly emergent and constructivist. No matter how much anyone else has studied an idea or mastered a skill, all professional educators have to make sense of those ideas and skills, both by themselves and through learning together, to become more expert. Sometimes developing new skills will mean learning to read situations and people in new ways and seeing the world with new eyes. Sometimes, despite the best intentions, without adequate reflection and feedback from others we simply cannot see what we are doing, nor can we see what some ideas are really all about or how some people think or some procedures work.

The materials or procedures or programs that are used with the process learning circles vary according to need. Sometimes the objective is to work through a subject-specific program of some sort, often at a certain grade level. The objective may address reading or math or science. Sometimes the focus may be a more general approach to learning and teaching (which is our emphasis). In other cases the emphasis may be on assessment, and on the best ways to gather information and ascertain results. At other times a specific problem may need to be dealt with, ranging from, say, issues of discipline and attendance to how to integrate mandated programs.

The processes described in this book can be modified to suit different circumstances. However, our focus is professional development and *not* problem solving. And so, from our perspective, every topic or issue that is addressed should *always* be dealt with as raw material to be learned from and used as a vehicle for increasing knowledge, developing skills, and generally increasing educators' real-world competence. For this reason, a key feature of this book is that *the procedures and principles are intended to be used during the teaching day and week, and are not just to be experienced during meetings and other staff sessions.*

Who This Book Is For

This book is intended to guide all those who lead or who participate in and support the development of professional learning communities. It provides tools for both. Sometimes the users of this book will be highly skilled group leaders, and sometimes not. The key is to discern and then use one's current strengths as a benchmark against which to develop and grow—and to see that the learning is as much an adventure as it is about specific actions and strategies.

The ultimate goal is to create the conditions in which students are most likely to succeed. In our experience, when the proper foundations for good community are laid for all the adults in a school, a natural indirect effect spreads to the classrooms themselves. So just by improving their own learning community, educators are improving the learning community for students. In addition, the individual phases involved in the process learning circles can be modified and used as practical tools in the classroom, where they also become a way for directly cultivating a much better learning community.

part I

Foundations in
Research

1

Foundations of
Professional Development

The illiterate of the 21st century will not be those who cannot read and write, but those who cannot learn, unlearn, and relearn.

—Alvin Toffler, author and futurist

Professional development is about learning.

Becoming more expert is essential in the best of times. This challenge applies to every profession, from neurosurgeons who are constantly having to be aware of new discoveries and master the latest methods, to football coaches who have to keep up with the times, to educators who are bombarded with findings from brain research as well as changes in every subject area in the curriculum. It is even more important in a turbulent world characterized by rapid social and economic changes that impinge directly on the lives of students everywhere. Educators, above all, must be—and be seen as—quintessential learners.

A key to success in any field is to capitalize on all the learning capacities with which human beings are endowed. That is why this book approaches professional development from the perspective of how people learn naturally.

How Do People Become More Expert—Really?

As you look back on your progress as an educator (or, indeed, with any other skill or in any other profession), remind yourself of what it actually took for you to become more skillful. Ask yourself these questions:

- What state of mind were you in as you learned? And if you experienced many states of mind, which were most helpful and which were most inhibiting?
- What combination of theory and experience was required?
- Did you always learn exactly what you needed from the first experience you had?

These are the sorts of questions that have to be answered in a general way to gain the insight necessary to have programs that work. And research and experience are also available to show the way.

The goal of this book is to create a process that helps educators learn both for understanding *and* for real-world performance. For that to happen, the process needs to tap into how people learn naturally because throughout the ages, real-world performance has always been grounded in natural learning.

An overall understanding of how people learn naturally emerges out of the brain/mind learning principles that we have been developing for nearly 20 years (Appendix A has a more detailed explanation of the principles and the process). The core point is that meaningful learning that leads to real change engages every aspect of a person. It is just as important to teach the whole adult as it is to teach the whole child.

It becomes clear from the brain/mind learning principles that professional development is also a personal matter. When we realize that emotions and relationships and personal beliefs are involved, then we have to grapple with the fact that in professional development two different but parallel processes are taking place all the time: professional learning and personal learning.

Professional learning deals with mastery of new ideas and information and the development of new skills. Personal learning deals with developing new ways of seeing things, acquiring new capacities, and even adjusting some attitudes and beliefs. The point is that some professional learning can occur only if adequate personal learning also takes place. One example has to do with asking questions. An excellent example was given to us by a colleague, who told us about Myron:

> Myron was a professional development junkie. He was very sincere. And he loved to hear the sound of his own voice. About three years into his career as a teacher he began to take "wait time" seriously. He quite proudly asked our colleague to observe him. And when she did, she did not know whether to laugh or cry. Myron would ask the class a question. And then he would count to seven (privately, he thought), while waiting for an answer. And as our colleague looked around she saw all the students silently counting to seven together. She knew and they knew that he was just waiting for a chance to talk! But her feedback to him made no impact at all. She saw him again about a year later, quite by accident. He said that he had been taking a personal development course, and he had been learning how impatient he used to be, and how good it was to be able to relax as things unfolded. Then he blushed and grinned. "I guess," he said, "that wait time doesn't work if you're not really waiting." (Anonymous personal communication, Oct. 10, 2008)

This example illustrates both a specific point and a general point. Two aspects of the skill of asking questions are to genuinely care about what others actually think, and to be truly patient enough for them to find their thoughts and ask their questions. And, more generally, every skill depends for its effectiveness on the right foundation of personal attributes and capacities. So successful professional learning depends upon successful personal learning. Thus the conditions and processes that are created need to be sustained and effective enough for both layers of development to occur.

The Three Critical Elements of Great Professional Development

Our experience over many years and the conclusions that emerge from the research on learning (Caine, G., & Caine, R., 2001; Caine, R., et al., 2008; summarized in Appendix A) suggest that the optimal conditions for professional development (and student learning in the classroom) require the continuous presence of three interactive elements:

• Relaxed alertness as the optimal state of mind in individuals and the community

• The orchestrated immersion of learners in complex experience in which the content (information, ideas, and skills) is embedded

• The active processing of experience

Relaxed Alertness as the Optimal State of Mind

Relaxed alertness is a blend of low threat and high challenge. When you walk into a school where relaxed alertness is the norm, you can feel the difference in terms of less rushing and yelling, even though movement and activity are pervasive. Staff and faculty are smiling and listening to each other, notwithstanding the pressures found in any school. A sense of interest and excitement in the work itself is evident.

The problem of threat, stress, and fear. We first encountered this issue in the work of Les Hart (2002). He coined the word "down-shifting" to describe what happens when people experience threat to the point of feeling helpless. He based his notion on the work of neuroscientist Paul MacLean (1978), who argued that when the survival response kicks in, functioning is driven by more primitive parts of the brain. In other words, the brain moves into automatic, often quick but unreflective responses, and higher-order thinking is compromised.

Although the term "downshifting" is ambiguous (because when a vehicle "downshifts" it is moving into a more powerful gear), the phenomenon has been confirmed. Some of the most useful research comes from LeDoux (1996), a neuroscientist who has examined the effect of fear on the brain. LeDoux suggests that the brain functions in two basic modes—a high road and a low road. The low road is the road of survival. It is triggered by stimuli that provoke fear (such as giving a talk in public, for some people). In these circumstances, the immediate responses are fight or flight. And here is the critical point: a person in that state tends to literally lose access to some parts of the brain that handle higher-order functioning. Some capacities to think and react just vanish! (This phenomenon is explained in more detail in Caine, R., & Caine, G., 2011.)

Another term that can be used to describe what happens when schools are overstressed is what Staw and colleagues call "threat rigidity." Olsen and Sexton (2009), citing Staw and colleagues, state the following:

> Threat rigidity is the theory that an organization, when perceiving itself under siege (i.e., threatened or in crisis), responds in identifiable ways: Structures tighten; centralized control increases; conformity is stressed; accountability and efficiency measures are emphasized; and alternative or innovative thinking is discouraged. (p. 15)

For an extended description of how fear can affect one location (San Diego), read Chapter 4 of *The Death and Life of the Great American School System* (Ravitch, 2010).

The promise of challenge and intrinsic motivation. The high road is radically different from the low road. Imagine, for instance, a person who loves public speaking and finds it exhilarating. Being in front of an audience is exciting. The person's repertoire of experience and cognitive capacity can be accessed. And so the response may be one of actively entering into the event and enjoying every aspect of it. What is immensely threatening to one person is exciting and challenging to another—and the state of mind affects the capacity to function and perform.

Several fields of research are converging to support the added efficacy of learners who are relaxed and alert. This includes research into self-efficacy (Bandura, 2000); resilience (Davies, 2002; Gillham, 2000); the state of flow (Csikszentmihalyi, 1990); and positive psychology in general (see, for example, Seligman, 1991). One example of research being conducted is a study on what is called "positive affect"—a mild increase in positive feelings. Positive affect has been shown to improve higher-order functions such as the following:

- Episodic and working memory
- Creative problem solving
- Social interactions (helpfulness and sociability)
- Decision making
- Flexibility in thinking
- Improved verbal fluency in adolescents (Ashby, Isen, & Turken, 1999)

One aspect of this positive mind state is intrinsic motivation, which emerges when learners have many opportunities to ask their *own* questions and deal with issues of personal interest. This was precisely the approach that was used in the first school we were ever asked to work in—Dry Creek Elementary, a small, K–6 school north of Sacramento, California. It was the early 1990s, and under the leadership of the principal, Cindy Tucker, the staff had spent several months examining alternatives and deciding on what to do to improve. One of them came across our book *Making Connections: Teaching and the Human Brain* (Caine, R., & Caine, G., 1994). Shortly after the staff had read it, we received a call from Cindy. She said (almost verbatim), "Hello. You haven't heard of me. We've been reading your book, and we'd like you to come and work with us." Geoffrey then flew to Sacramento to discuss a possible program. Much of the process described in this book was either developed or clarified as a result of the five years that we spent working with Dry Creek.

At the other end of the spectrum, we have also frequently been called in to meet with staff who have been instructed—irrespective of what they want or think or feel—to meet and work with us. The difference in attitude on first meeting compared with our experience in Dry Creek is striking—and, for the most part, so are the results. The lesson here is that it is important to have buy-in from participants, that they be open to enjoying the process, to being interested in becoming more effective, to actually looking forward to trying out new things and learning from mistakes as well as successes, and to exploring and discussing all this with colleagues in a safe environment.

Participants in a good learning community find that it helps to have colleagues with whom to talk things through, reflect, analyze, and discuss. In fact, when the right procedures are used, the community can end up being an oasis of safety in which high-level, in-depth learning takes place. Thus, the foundation for developing relaxed alertness is an orderly (but not rigid) and caring community, with healthy relationships based on respectful and coherent procedures.

The Orchestrated Immersion of Learners in Complex Experience

Science is now explaining what everyday life has confirmed over centuries and what is almost certainly true in your personal experience: natural learning is not just an intellectual process. If a person is learning how to read situations in new ways (a shift in perceptual capacities), such as seeing the order and collaboration in some types of "messy" classrooms, and is acquiring new skills for real-world performance, then body, brain, and mind must all be engaged in the learning. (See Appendix A for a brief comment on the relationship between brain and mind.) The whole person learns, which requires a constant combination of academic content and practical experience. That is the essence of orchestrated immersion.

More specifically, participants need opportunities to do the following activities:

• Analyze, and sometimes research, the material in question

   • Have opportunities to link new material to what they already know
   • Take action and physically engage with material to be mastered or understood
   • Receive coaching, guidance, and explanations
   • Observe competent performances by others
   • Use the material as the basis for action in the real world

This range of activities should not be surprising. Young children mastering their native language or culture are exposed to all of these aspects of experience, as is anyone who becomes an expert in any field, ranging from scientific research to sports.

   Similarly, a professional development program must include a range of experiences that extend beyond study, intellectual analysis, and conversation to actually trying things out in the classroom and the laboratory. It is only through experience that people get a feel for what they are trying to do or become, and that they see how things actually happen. Test this assertion in your own experience, returning to the questions we asked earlier. Have you ever mastered a complex new skill without actually trying it out several times, in various ways, in the real world? The key is to make the process manageable, systematic, and sustained over time.

The Active Processing of Experience

   It is all well and good to try things out, but the exercise bears fruit only when people intentionally and systematically learn from their experience. Experience needs to be digested, or processed, which is why Schön's books (1990, 1995) on what he calls "the reflective practitioner" are still useful, and why it is important to combine reflection *on* action (which occurs afterward) and reflection *in* action (which occurs in the moment). Many others have written about reflective practice, describing recent developments (e.g., Larrivee & Cooper, 2005; Osterman & Kottkamp, 2004), proposing a greater focus on metacognition (e.g., Perfect & Schwartz, 2002), and providing guidance on reflective practice for learning communities (Collay, Dunlap, Enloe, & Gagnon, 1998).

Constant, ongoing active processing is thus the third indispensable element for optimal professional development. The key for those who are conducting programs of professional development is to go beyond providing information to ensuring that participants have many opportunities to receive feedback, digest, think about, question, examine, and process what they are experiencing—guided by process leaders. Active processing includes, where appropriate, activities such as these:

- Detailed observation of actions and responses
- Deliberate (selective and mindful) practice and rehearsal
- Multiple modes of questioning
- Analysis of data and sources
- Ongoing responses to and reflection on feedback
- Expansion of capacities for self-discipline and self-regulation

Active processing is doubly useful because it simultaneously provides feedback for process leaders and also can be used to expand and deepen participants' thinking. In this way, active processing resembles some aspects of formative assessment in the classroom, providing useful information for both leader (teacher) and participants (students) as instruction and learning proceed.

As a practical matter, the questioning aspect of active processing is complex, because there are so many ways to ask questions that the whole experience can be overwhelming. After this became apparent to us in our work with Dry Creek, we found that a good approach is to begin with just four questions (all asked in the spirit of inquiry and not of criticism):

- Can you tell me what you are doing?
- Why did you decide to do it this way?
- Can you explain it?
- What would happen if you changed one element (such as...)?

Professional Development Revisited

The three elements described here ensure that any learner—student or staff member—is being guided to make sense of things on an individual level. The three-part approach makes certain that theory translates into practice and that intellectual understanding becomes real-world competence. Many programs fall flat if participants are not in the appropriate state of mind, if the programs are characterized by too much talk and not enough walk, or if the activities are not adequately processed or "mined" for all the learning and possible meanings they may contain.

The three elements and their components do not need to occur in a linear or sequential fashion. Rather, they should be seen as a triple helix, with each element supporting and being a part of the other two. In this way professional development becomes dynamic and continuous. The primary indicator of success is the fact that educators have spontaneous conversations about theory and practice outside session hours and begin to try things out on their own initiative. Their learning then takes on a life of its own.

2

Effective Learning Communities

The new kind of community building is not an event; it is a process.
—*Beth Jarman and George Land,*
"Beyond Breakpoint: Possibilities for a New Community"

Cast your mind back to a time when you sat somewhere (say, a coffee shop) and discussed work with a couple of friends, comparing notes and occasionally making suggestions about actions to take. You may also have done the same by phone or online. When this happened you were a participant in a community of learners.

Of course, there are different kinds of communities, and not all conversations lead to useful learning. The point, however, is that although people vary in how much they like to learn and work together, the brain/mind is social. Learning in the real world has always been a partially social process. We see this, for instance, in the fact that children play together at being adults in every society in the world.

The social nature of learning has been demonstrated by research in psychology, sociology, and organizational development. Cognitive psychologists (e.g., Lave & Wenger, 1991) use the term "situated cognition" to describe learning that is "situated" in a social context. Bank tellers, new parents, doctors, baseball players, journalists, and others pick up part of what they do and much of their understanding of their roles and jobs through conversations with, interactions with, and observations of their peers. Similarly, every teacher and administrator is in constant social contact with colleagues, parents, district office staff, and others, and these relationships affect their understanding of what happens in school. System theorists argue, in fact, that an organization itself may learn (Senge, 2006) and that one of the best steps for improving an organization is to set it up so that conditions make it easier for individuals to learn more effectively.

In fact, it is now known that the social nature of people is embedded in their biology. In the 1980s and 1990s, neuroscientist Giacomo Rizzolatti and his colleagues (2008) discovered mirror neurons—nerve cells in the brains of observing animals that fire in a similar way to nerve cells of animals that they are observing. The neuron "'mirrors' the behavior of another animal, as though the observer were itself acting" (Wikipedia, which we use regularly as a quick and very useful introductory way of researching a host of topics). This applies to human beings as well as to animals. So the capacity for imitation and empathy is actually built into all of us and is a key to how we pick up our native culture and language (although who we imitate and whether empathy is reinforced or diminished are complex matters).

Types of Learning Communities

Learning together in groups can occur in many different ways, all having certain strengths and weaknesses, and all offering something from which we can borrow. Four to consider are study groups, action research teams, communities of practice, and conversation circles. In addition, online communication is facilitating new kinds of shared learning.

Study Groups

When people have the same material to study, it can be useful to do so together. A study group is essentially a reading and discussion group. Participants usually read material ahead of time and then analyze it collectively when they meet. University students do this often, and it is common in self-directed study groups, used extensively in countries such as Sweden (Oliver, 1987). In schools, the process tends to be used by teachers who teach a common subject, but it is often useful to create whole-faculty study groups (Murphy & Lick, 2004). In fact, one of the best ways to prepare for an in-depth, schoolwide program of professional development is to spend time as a study group to evaluate the research, experience, and processes that are being advocated in any particular project or approach. Dry Creek Elementary had taken these steps before contacting us (see Chapter 1). One challenge for study groups lies in the material that is selected, which may vary from the trivial to the highly abstract, and in the makeup of the groups, whose members may vary widely in how much they already know and understand.

Action Research Teams

Action research has been explored vigorously for several decades (see, e.g., Reason & Bradbury, 2007). Briefly, it involves taking action in a real-world setting, reflecting on the experience, discussing the implications with colleagues, and then perhaps taking additional action based on the conclusions drawn. It generally uses systematic procedures to learn from experience. Here is a simple definition from Wikipedia: "Action research is a reflective process of progressive problem solving led by individuals working with others in teams... to improve the way they address issues and solve problems."

It is absolutely essential to try things in real-world settings and then take the time to learn from that experience. This aspect of the PrLC process ensures that participants take action systematically and reflect on it. So there needs to be a discussion about implications for practice, a decision to take some action, and procedures for learning adequately from the action taken. In a very general sense, that is what we mean by action research.

Action research can involve a variety of approaches and goals. One type of action research occurs when a group of educators work together to identify a problem, develop a strategy to solve it, and research their own results (Brighton, 2009). For example, a common problem is lack of parental involvement with children's education. We enjoyed watching teachers from one school with which we worked, puzzling over the problem and talking about it for months. One of them, who was also a parent, was invited to attend a teacher-parent-student conference with her son and her son's teacher in which her son led the conference. During the conversation, she had the insight that other parents, like her, might value such meetings. She shared the idea with her colleagues, who unanimously agreed to try it the next semester. Their sense after the trial was that the innovation was successful in at least increasing parents' awareness of, and interest in, what their children were studying and how they were doing. And the process (which grows and changes with experience) continues to this day.

Another focus of action research may be on collecting data to help educators see what is actually happening in a school. Collecting measurable data is complex because data come in many different forms, but it is extremely important. Data collection is at the heart of a process developed by the DuFours (DuFour, Eaker, & DuFour, 2008) and is the basis of what they call professional learning communities.

A third approach is for individuals to experiment with new strategies in their classrooms and then to reflect on their own experiences and what they discover about their own beliefs, mental models, and practices. This is a central thrust of reflective practice (Schön, 1990, 1995). One of the teachers at Dry Creek did precisely that when she decided she wanted to get better at telling and using stories. She began simply, tried things out, noticed how her students reacted, and improved accordingly. That success became the launching pad for a marvelous improvement in her overall teaching.

Action research can vary widely in the specificity of what is researched and in the degree of rigor that is involved. In our example of the parent-teacher-student conference, for example, much of the development occurred as a result of trial and error that was ongoing but not very systematic. Much more sophisticated approaches are possible, but in our experience, even less rigorous processes can work well.

Communities of Practice

In recent years it has become clear that much of what people learn about their jobs and professions is picked up informally from conversations with their colleagues and others. Lave and Wenger (1991) coined the term "communities of practice" to explain this phenomenon. Their initial research was with clerks who processed claims in insurance offices. They observed that the forms were complex, and information from claimants was not always easy to understand. They also observed numerous times when one clerk would turn to another and ask what to do. In this way, the clerks had developed their own informal community of mutual instruction and help—a community of practice. Lave and Wenger show that this approach works across many fields, from bank tellers and insurance clerks to expert biologists and researchers. And, of course, it occurs throughout the world of education, when teachers talk about certain students or how to work with a particular parent or what to do about a new form of assessment. Wenger and his colleagues have essentially taken the best of what they found in informal processes and organized it into a more systematic structure that others can use, developing what has now become one of the most powerful and influential modes of training and development in business (Wenger, McDermott, & Snyder, 2002).

Communities of practice spring up wherever people work together. The informal learning that takes place is both a strength and a weakness, because people share what they do and know and currently believe—which means that they could be sharing good practice or bad practice.

Conversation Circles

The term "conversation circles" describes a practice that has roots in many different traditions. It is the practice of being seated in a circle and using certain routines and procedures to make it easier for people to deal with difficult issues, to be able to speak their truth, and to be heard. Many indigenous peoples use some form of circle. It is similar in many ways to procedures followed in the intellectual salons of 19th century Europe. Other groups such as the Quakers, while not necessarily seated in a circle, use similar processes to ensure that each person has an opportunity to speak and to be fully heard. And several processes in vogue today operate in similar ways (see some of the examples at the end of the section on deep listening in Appendix B).

One challenge with conversation circles is that they can vary enormously in the superficiality or depth of discussion. Our process assumes that all procedures will begin in a fairly superficial way and that as participants become more comfortable and proficient, the conversations and processes will deepen.

Communicating Online

New technologies have radically expanded the opportunities for people to communicate, and with that has come an explosion in the use of different types of online communities, ranging from closed groups to discussion forums to loosely bounded social networks such as those on Facebook. This technological capacity is both a blessing and a burden. On the one hand, it helps and supports some of the procedures described in this book. On the other hand, many people feel that online interaction can replace the face-to-face experience. Sometimes it can; often it can't. In Appendix D we introduce some of the online capacities that are available and that can be extraordinarily useful. However, they are only a supplement to professional learning groups, whose goals include creating a greater sense of community in the face-to-face world, and developing practical competence (which also depends upon taking action in the real world).

A Field of Listening

What is it like to be heard? And what is it like to *not* be heard?

Hearing each other is crucial for building relationships. And an indispensable key to the success of all types of effective learning communities is that they be grounded in good relationships, where the participants hear and feel they are heard. Permeating such communities is a good "field of listening."

A field is a shared space that is also a region of mutual influence. A field of listening is one that is permeated by the spirit of listening—where the core assumption is that fully listening to others is the appropriate thing to do. The field begins with pleasant relationships. When the field deepens, however, it goes beyond nice to authentic. It is the space where we can feel strongly and yet be unattached to our own opinions, where we can give and receive effective feedback without putting our egos on the line and can begin to function at a higher level with less effort. In this space we do not need to battle to feel heard, and feeling heard is one of the core ingredients in authentic communication.

Success with others in every sphere of education—from the staff room to the classroom, from the district office to the parent conference—depends on being able to listen effectively. That is why one of Stephen Covey's seven habits of effective people is to "seek first to understand, then to be understood" (2004).

The alternative was powerfully illustrated in the research program that examined threat rigidity, introduced in Chapter 1. Olsen and Sexton (2009) followed six teachers in a large high school code-named Hawthorne, as the school and the teachers tried to deal with external mandates and internal issues. Processes such as small learning communities were imposed without adequate teacher voice; some members of staff were favorites with administrators, so that a small group had, in fact, a very loud voice. The teachers reported that they did not feel heard by administrators. Tensions developed within groups and beyond groups, and teachers retreated to their classrooms and felt isolated. The researchers reported psychological stress, intergroup and intragroup difficulties, defensiveness and resentment, and a desire to hide one's practice.

As this counterexample illustrates, one of the core ingredients in building community and a sense of safety and commitment is for the participants to feel heard. We expand upon the field of listening in more depth in Appendix B.

Process Learning Circles

The process learning circle (PrLC) format integrates key aspects of all of the types of learning community described earlier. It has two primary objectives. The first is to create a field of listening as the foundation for learning and working together in a stimulating and inviting climate. The better the atmosphere in a school, the easier it is to deal with the host of problems that confront every educator and, at the same time, to make sure that the work continues to be enjoyable. Time and again we see people who grasp the fact that the key to success is relationship. Thus in an interview in the *Tennessean*, a new associate superintendent for high schools in Nashville said the following:

> It's about relationships. Being a band teacher, you form relationships with kids that go beyond the classroom. You form relationships with the community—you're working with large groups of kids and parents, and you're providing experiences that will last a lifetime for a group of kids. It's the same concept in redesigning high schools. (Sarrio, 2009)

The second objective is to act more specifically as a vehicle to help educators become more proficient—more expert—so that they are better equipped to facilitate the learning of their students, irrespective of age and grade, gender, ethnicity, social and economic circumstances, giftedness, or any other factor. Our approach was formalized in the work we did with Dry Creek Elementary in the 1990s, and was first published in *Mindshifts* (Caine et al., 1999).

We continue to research and implement the PrLC procedure. For example, it was used in a successful one-year program with a low–socioeconomic status school in Fontana, California, in 2001 (Caine, R., 2008), which we describe in some detail in Chapter 11. A news-paper story several years later reported that the results there were still being maintained (Hartmann, 2006).

The process has been enriched as we have discovered more about the basic biological and psychological nature of learning. And those of us who use the format have benefited enormously from the experiences of others who have tried it, ranging from informal evening meetings of six or seven parents to large-scale, whole-district projects with which we have been involved.

We should note that the process also operates at a deeper level than what we describe in these pages. An interaction always occurs between individuals and a group—to some extent each actually shapes the other. People come to think and feel and perceive and act differently in response to the communities that they find themselves in and that they help to create (see, for example, Barab & Duffy, 2000). Thus it is important to proactively participate in creating a dynamic learning environment for the adults in a school.

The Larger Picture

We have focused here on individual PrLCs. However, such groups operate within the larger school or organizational community, and the ultimate goal is to create a learning community in the school or organization as a whole. Ideally, the place where people go to work should be suffused with positive feelings, with most relationships at least cordial and professional. Creating such a place requires paying attention to ways of connecting and integrating the smaller PrLCs into a larger framework (we address that issue in Chapter 13, which deals with group dynamics).

Figure 2.1 is a general survey that you can use to assess the learning climate in your current school community. It refers to "downshifting" and "threat rigidity," which, you'll recall from Chapter 1, are terms related to the effect that stress has on people and institutions, including schools. Your responses to the survey questions will be colored by your state of mind at the moment, and you may also answer differently at different times of the year. Nevertheless, answering the questions will provide you with a good general sense of your workplace's climate and state of community. The exercise can be used in several different ways. We find it extremely useful as the basis for one or more meetings of the PrLCs.

Figure 2.1
Assessing the Learning Climate in the School Community

Directions: Circle Yes or No for each question. Specific answers may not be critical, but generally, more Yes's in Sections 1 and 2, combined with more No's in Section 3, indicate a greater likelihood that downshifting or threat rigidity is occurring. Note that in recording your responses, it does not matter how much control you have over the situation. In fact, the less control or input you feel that you have, the more likely you are to experience downshifting yourself.

**1. Factors That Indicate Downshifting
in the Learning/Teaching Process**

Yes No Letter or number grades are the primary means of
         evaluation.

Yes No Curriculum is fragmented, with subjects separated from
         each other and from life.

Yes No Classrooms are organized by age/grade.

Yes No Most outcomes are prespecified by teachers in the form
         of behavioral objectives.

Yes No Focus on alternative answers and solutions is lacking.

Figure 2.1 (*continued*)

Assessing the Learning Climate in the School Community

Yes No   Language and math are highly emphasized, with little focus on other capacities or intelligences.

Yes No   Teaching shows general indifference to learning styles.

Yes No   Group participation is lacking.

Yes No   Staff are generally indifferent to student interests and how they relate to subject matter.

Yes No   Staff are indifferent to student experiences as rich sources of connection to the focus of the curriculum.

Yes No   Motivation is largely determined by rewards and punishments.

Yes No   Class time is dominated by the teacher (a "delivery model" of teaching prevails).

Yes No   Bells, announcements, and other interruptions are constant.

Yes No   Fixed time schedules govern the length and duration of learning tasks.

Yes No   Teachers lack planning time.

Yes No   The curriculum is prescribed, not faculty generated or developed by faculty/educator teams.

2. Factors That Indicate Downshifting in the School Generally

Yes No   Staff are divided into factions.

Yes No   Resistance to change is extensive.

Yes No   Negativity is extensive.

Yes No   Concern for the system as a whole is limited.

Yes No   Burnout is prevalent.

Yes No   Staff operate with few teacher teams or partnerships.

Yes No   Faculty are expected to be accountable but have no power.

Yes No   Student apathy is common.

Yes No   Student absenteeism is frequent.

Yes No   Staff absenteeism is frequent.

Figure 2.1 (*continued*)

Assessing the Learning Climate in the School Community

3. Some Factors That Counter Downshifting

Yes No Students participate in their own evaluation (including assessment of their own strengths and weaknesses).

Yes No Students are given choices on tasks.

Yes No Tasks are related to student goals, concerns, and interests.

Yes No Tasks incorporate student experiences.

Yes No Tasks include open-ended assignments.

Yes No Student creativity is engaged and encouraged.

Yes No Teachers help students process "deep meanings" (the implications of content on their own values, drives, purposes).

Yes No Many time lines are flexible and linked to activities.

Yes No Time is provided for student-teacher conferencing.

Yes No Time is provided for teacher-teacher conferencing.

Yes No Time is provided for teacher-student-parent conferencing.

Yes No "Mistakes" are seen as a natural aspect of learning.

Yes No Students share and work with each other.

Yes No Students engage in reflection on content and on themselves (active processing).

part II

How to Conduct Process Learning Circles

3

The Process
Learning Circle Format

The whole is greater than the sum of the parts.

Process learning circles generate a field of listening while implementing the three elements of professional learning described in Chapter 1. As you'll recall, those elements are the following:

• Relaxed alertness as the optimal state of mind in individuals and the community
• The orchestrated immersion of learners in complex experience in which the content (information, ideas, and skills) is embedded
• The active processing of experience

The complete PrLC procedure is partly linear and structured, in that each meeting has a precise number of phases (four) and each phase has some essential ingredients. However, it also allows for dynamism and change and individual differences.

Each phase can stand alone as an individual process, powerful in its own right. Based on what is now known about how people learn, we suggest that all four need to be present somewhere, in some systematic way, in any effective program of professional development.

Process Learning Circles in Context

Although short talks and single days of inservice training can provide some benefits, it is clear that effective professional development takes time. In fact, professional development should be ongoing. We suggest that a program with a specific focus should usually last for at least a year.

Professional learning circles are the fulcrum—the central leverage point—of this ongoing professional development process. The learning circles need to meet frequently enough to build relationships and to sustain learning. For that reason, we suggest holding a two-hour meeting at least twice a month.

The groups are suitable for any adult working in or with a school or larger educational unit. Most commonly participants are teachers and administrators. However, invitations to participate can be extended to special resource personnel, librarians, psychologists, secretaries, custodians, and teacher aides, as we did with Dry Creek Elementary, provided the content is appropriate and useful.

The reason for including all members of staff is that every adult contributes to the community that is created for children, and children learn from every adult. Ideally, all adults should have a common mental model of how people learn, their roles and functions should be mutually reinforcing, and they should all be contributors to the community. For instance, a positive and pleasant atmosphere in the school office and on the playground indirectly helps all teachers maintain orderliness and build a good learning environment in their classrooms.

In general, we suggest that the participants should be volunteers. The reason is that they will be discussing beliefs, sharing practices, revealing uncertainties and doubts, and reflecting on experiences that could have been joyful but also challenging. Participants need to be willing to do that.

The Structure of Process Learning Circles

As the name implies, process learning circles are structured with people seated in a circle, which reduces any sense of hierarchy and makes it easy for everyone to see and hear everyone else. A process leader guides the group. This person can be an "outside" consultant or a member of the circle. And sometimes leadership rotates, for reasons discussed later.

Each two-hour meeting has four phases, which we briefly describe here. Each phase is also discussed in more depth in one of the chapters that follows.

Phase 1: Ordered Sharing (10–15 Minutes)

Primary purpose: Initiate a field of listening.

This activity calls for each participant to respond to a question or a short, powerful saying introduced by the group leader (see Chapter 5 for some examples). Each shares a personal story, a thought, or a reflection. The sharing continues around the circle, with each person speaking in turn. Everyone pays full attention to each speaker without interruption. This is the core process for developing listening skills and building the atmosphere of respectful listening and relaxed alertness that is so essential to the process.

Phase 2: Reflective Study (1 Hour)

Primary purpose: Understand and personalize core ideas.

In this phase new material for the session is introduced. This can be done in different ways (see Chapter 6), but in any case, it is extremely important during this phase to examine the material intellectually *and* personally. In other words, the core ideas and skills need to be analyzed and discussed, and participants should also bring to mind personal experiences that seem to be related and raise questions of personal or professional relevance. During this phase, the discussion is open and need not go around the circle.

Phase 3: Commitment to Action and Action Research (25 Minutes)

Primary purpose: Learn by doing and reflecting.

Now is the time for participants, either individually or in discussion with others, to decide on, and to commit to, actually using some aspect of the material in the following weeks. The commitment is written down. Each participant talks briefly about what she plans to do, and the ordered-sharing format of Phase 1 can be used if desired. The participants will then take some action, and the results will be the basis for some reflection at the next meeting of the process learning circle. This is a simple but effective introduction to action research.

Phase 4: Regrouping (10–15 Minutes)
Primary purpose: Consolidate the learnings from the meeting itself.

Phase 4 is an opportunity to reflect on the session itself and on one's own participation—and then to share some critical learning. Participants may focus on the core content and themes that emerged for them as a way to develop content mastery. Or participants may use the time to get a handle on how well they listen, on how effectively they communicate, on their facility with questioning, and on many other capacities and practices, just from being aware of their own responses and participation in the circle. As this phase brings the session to a close, it is also generally done in the form of an ordered sharing.

Expanded Format

We have successfully used the process described without variation from meeting to meeting. A way to make it more powerful, however, is to shift the emphasis of the second meeting in the month. The increased power comes about because the more active exploration that teachers do with new strategies and processes in their classrooms, the more they need to work together to talk through what is happening and what they are learning. In these circumstances, we recommend that participants continue to meet twice a month, but that the format for the second meeting be more heavily weighted toward reporting on and processing their two weeks of classroom experiences with the new material or processes. (At the first meeting, new material is introduced and the format is exactly as described earlier.) Because the purpose of the midmonth meeting is to help participants expand on what they are learning from practice, feedback will occupy more time at the second meeting of the month than at the first. (See Chapter 7 for more information on the commitment to action and action research.)

An Effective Structure

Because some of the processes of the learning circles may be unfamiliar, they may feel uncomfortable at first. The benefit is that they set the stage for joyful, powerful, and effective sessions in the longer term—and that is the foundation for successful professional development.

Over time, groups find their own rhythm. However, it is extremely important to adhere to the structure and guidelines presented here for enough meetings to ensure that the spirit and integrity of the process become natural.

The protocols help to build a container—a space within which the process happens. Containers have boundaries (though they can be quite porous). And containers have a location in space and time. The very fact of putting these protocols in place helps to provide support and stability for the process that is to take place.

Often groups have come together under the guise of a process learning circle to simply chat. For instance, in the mid-1990s we had introduced the process to a district in Michigan, and several people from the district office let us know that they were meeting regularly as a result of our work. Geoffrey was invited back two years later for more advanced work. Two facts quickly became clear. First, the participants loved and valued their time together. And second, they had ignored the process almost completely. This was not quite the flexibility we had in mind! Meeting to chat is an important and legitimate reason to get together—but just chatting interferes with the depth that makes these circles magical.

The format can be adjusted in multiple ways, but the indispensable and central point is that the core phases need to be maintained if the process is to work. Each of the four phases is essential because, together, they ensure that all the essential elements of powerful learning are included in a program of *ongoing* professional development. The objective is to create a field of listening, explore essential ideas and skills in a conceptual and experiential way, commit to real-world action, and then to process and learn from experience. The combination of elements, together with the emphasis on hearing each other and working together, begins to build an *authentic professional learning community* over time.

4

Logistics

Nothing is a waste of time if you use the experience wisely.

—*Auguste Rodin*

When a process learning circle is dealing with an issue that directly affects the entire community in, say, a school, we suggest that all adults have the option of participating, including teachers, administrators, and nonteaching staff. Such an approach deepens the collective understanding, which, in turn, can lead to more coherent—and more effective—procedures and practices. As we noted, the atmosphere in the school office and on the playground sets much of the tone for the experiences that students have in school.

Our experience is that groups function best when some of the participants do not work together too closely outside the circle format (e.g., in grade-level clusters or subject-matter groupings). Variety and novelty of input expands our horizons. However, the more a process focuses on specific instructional material, the more likely it is that participants will be those with a direct interest in the area.

Administrative Details

Some basic mechanics always need to be addressed, and although it is helpful to be able to deal with them all ahead of time, in practice that is not always possible. For instance, the location for meetings may have to change at the last minute, or a person who seemed to be really committed to the effort suddenly becomes unavailable. These are just facts of life to be handled as the circumstances warrant. The important thing is to be clear about the basics and to cover them as much as possible.

Volunteers

Again, we emphasize the importance of group participants being volunteers because that lays the groundwork for a safe environment for sharing. In these groups, adults take responsibility for expressing opinions and publicly engaging in personal learning. Personal disclosure involves a certain amount of risk, even if we just have to reveal to our colleagues what we do or do not know about learning theory and research. People will be seen to be at different developmental stages in their own professional growth. Individual strengths and weaknesses will become apparent. In these circumstances, it is vital that the people who engage in the process choose to do so willingly. This may be difficult, especially if some people feel pressure to participate and pretend to volunteer. Our advice is that, for the most part, no one should participate out of pressure, and no one should employ threat to induce participation. To do so is to invite sabotage of the process, which can lead to unhappiness for everyone. Those who participate willingly are likely to find that they have embarked on a personal and professional growth process that is both challenging and deeply fulfilling.

Of course, like most rules, this one has possible exceptions. Here are some examples:

> In one example, the director of professional development in a school district insisted that every school administrator—principals and their deputies and assistants—participate. She believed that administrators had so much responsibility for the students that their presence should be mandated. Although there were some initial grumblings, an independent research study commissioned by her showed that the process was very effective in building communication at the administrator level. (J. Stevens, personal communication, 1996)

In another example, Dry Creek Elementary implemented the process systematically for some time, and it had become part of the practice as a way of building and sustaining a good culture and learning community. In those circumstances, the principal wanted new teachers joining the staff to participate in the process to fully understand and become a part of the school's way of operating.

As these examples show, the rule about volunteers cannot be absolute, but there should be a good reason for making participation in the process learning circle mandatory.

Group Size

The ideal number of participants in a PrLC is about 6 to 10. Our research indicates that when a group has more than 10 people, the process is less effective, in part because a larger number of participants prevents each person from having enough time to express individual thoughts and opinions. And when the number falls below about 7, the energy level tends to drop and the opinions expressed don't offer enough variety.

However, we realize that sometimes size might vary from our recommendation. For instance, a group may have as many as 18 to 20 participants, particularly if time is limited and only one person is the key process leader. In these circumstances, we suggest that a leader have at least some practice or experience with the process as recommended before beginning to experiment with other permutations and combinations, such as the larger group size mentioned here. It is also possible to go to the other extreme: Just two people can work the process well.

Location

Because the purpose of the group is to engage in reflective learning and not be caught up in everyday issues, we suggest that, whenever possible, you meet away from your normal workplace. Doing so reduces the number of reminders about work-related matters and the number of interruptions to the meeting.

Sometimes people might meet at private homes. If this is the case, we suggest that you rotate homes so that everyone is both a host and a guest. We also strongly suggest that you do not regard this as a time when you have to entertain people or go out of your way to provide a lot of food and beverages.

On occasion, it is simply not possible to meet outside the workplace. If that is the case, you might meet in a room in a part of the school or district where you seldom find yourself. Simply choose a place that enables you to function peacefully, comfortably, and without interruption as much as possible. If you will be meeting in a staff room or classroom, we suggest that everyone help to clean the room and make it orderly. Put books on shelves, arrange chairs in a circle, and make sure that other furniture is out of the way. Generally prepare the environment so that, as much as possible, it can take people out of the day-to-day feeling of being in school.

One principal has taken this idea much further. He has started to place old leather furniture in the foyer. He has brought in fresh plants and has hung prints of great works of art on the wall. He finds that parents, staff, and students love spending time in what used to be a place to pass through. That kind of approach is what we have in mind when setting up the meeting space for the PrLC.

Time and Duration

In an ideal situation, when the time is available, we recommend that you meet at least twice a month for two hours at a time. Again, modification may be necessary. For instance, in one school, it became obvious that meetings could be held for only about one and a half hours, but this worked well.

It is important, of course, to allow for some transitional time so that participants can finish the business of the day and then shift focus to the group in a fresh way.

Process Leaders

In the early stages of the PrLC, some natural leaders may stand out. It is appropriate for someone who is both acceptable to the participants and who has undeniably good process skills to lead the overall proceedings for some weeks or months. However, the goal is for everyone to be both a leader and a follower. Meeting this goal is critical to establishing mutual respect and overcoming the tendency for social and professional status to interfere with genuine communication. That is why we suggest that after the first few meetings, group leadership should rotate.

Getting Started

There is no one right way to start a process learning circle. Sometimes one or two teachers may read one of our other books or look at our website and decide that they want to form a group. A school or district may have an inservice session on brain/mind learning, and a principal or curriculum director may organize groups. A school may embark on a long-term restructuring program, and the staff may find out about and then vote on using the PrLC format. Sometimes a small group within a school may form a PrLC and then explain it to others who have seen it working for a while.

In one instance, two K–2 teachers at a school in California, both with an arts background, discovered the process from one of our books and simply began to use it between the two of them. They were enthusiastic and were obviously succeeding with their students, and so the principal suggested that they make a presentation to the whole school. At the end of that presentation, several members of staff were interested and then formed a PrLC, which was cofacilitated by the two teachers who had initiated the process.

A Structured Beginning

When we are called to a school to launch a PrLC, we conduct an intensive one- or two-day workshop. Sometimes it is for process leaders only, other times for the entire staff. During that workshop, everyone experiences the entire process at least twice, which gives both participants and process leaders a frame of reference and a foundation for the future.

When the group has a leader or coach with sufficient experience and expertise, conducting a one-day introductory workshop is nevertheless a good way to set the process in motion and help people gain a sense of what they are getting into. The PrLCs are often formed at the end of this day.

The First Meeting

If you can't conduct an introductory workshop, just begin at the beginning without worrying about following every step precisely. The process may feel strange at first, and people will also have different opinions as to what, exactly, the guidelines do or do not permit. One way to deal with the unfamiliarity is to make the first meeting a trial run. Follow the procedural guidelines as best you can, but do not pay too much attention to any real content. One option would be to use the material describing the PrLC format as your content. This will give participants and leaders an opportunity to get a feel for the process and to have a sense of how it will unfold over, say, a two-hour period. You can also use this meeting to discuss logistical issues, implications for practice, and commitment to the process; to make plans for the next few months (or an entire year); and to generally get prepared. We strongly recommend that you begin with an ordered sharing, and that during the conversations you practice allowing others to speak and listen to what is said.

The principal requirement is that people commit to a program of at least several months, and that they take some time to gain an idea of what they are embarking upon. They can do this through various means, including reading, informal discussion, or formal inservice sessions.

Selecting Issues to Explore

Selecting the right issue to explore is critical to good professional development, and leaders face a variety of potential problems in this area. Sometimes programs are mandated that allow for little or no private learning and individual initiative. Sometimes schools engage in so many mandated (or self-selected) programs that not enough time is available in what is already a very limited amount of time for professional development. And sometimes mandated programs and materials are simply incompatible, calling for conflicting practices based on differing basic assumptions about how people learn and what great teaching looks like. The selection of appropriate materials is a challenging issue, and we address it in more depth in Chapter 10.

→| |← →| |← →| |← →| |←

At the end of this chapter you'll find a checklist for initiating process learning circles, as well as the first of a series of vignettes that illustrate, in simple terms, how a sample process learning circle can function. Although, as noted earlier, we recommend a group size of 6 to 10, the vignettes feature comments from only a few people—just enough to show the gist of what happens.

Checklist for Logistics

1. Handle administrative details.
- Plan on a process for identifying volunteers.
- Clarify group size and, if necessary, number of groups.
- Select a location.
- Plan time and duration of meetings.
- Identify process leaders.

2. Start the process.

• Plan a structured inservice session to start the process.

• Plan the first meeting, anticipating that the process might not be very precise.

3. Select issues to explore.

• Have a moderately clear purpose in mind before the process begins.

→| |← →| |← →| |← →| |←

The PrLC at Spring Valley School

The initial efforts of the school's PrLC have been directed toward the logistics of getting the group started. The group has decided to spend the year studying how people learn. They have chosen two chapters from *The Brain, Education, and the Competitive Edge* (Caine, G., & Caine, R., 2001) as their core reading, to be supplemented with other material from time to time. The principal has found a way for them to have the time to meet for two hours on every other Friday afternoon (that is, usually twice a month), in a corner of the school library.

Each of the participants has a copy of this book and the book that will be their primary source material. They also have a printed schedule of meetings and know that every effort will be made to stick to the schedule. The process leader for at least the first three sessions will be the assistant vice principal.

5

Ordered Sharing

You cannot truly listen to anyone and do anything else at the same time.

—M. Scott Peck

The first purpose of the ordered sharing phase is to initiate and sustain a field of listening within the process learning circle. It is critical that every participant have enough time to speak and be able to speak without being interrupted. The ordered sharing is a way to establish that practice, and it has a carryover effect to the rest of the circle meeting, even during ordinary conversation and discussion.

Over time, other developments evolve from the ordered sharing, including the following:

• As participants realize that enough time is allotted for everyone, they stop competing for time and begin to develop the patience required for genuine listening.

• As participants hear a greater variety of viewpoints without interruption and come to understand the foundations of those viewpoints, they begin to listen with less judgment—both of others and of themselves.

• During this process and the learning that occurs, participants begin to get a feel for "beginner's mind" (described later in the chapter)—the notion that the key to learning is often to change one's own mind, and so less attachment to one's own current beliefs is desirable.

Thus a field of listening and a culture of learning are seeded and nourished.

The Process

We find it useful to describe the process of ordered sharing as a series of simple steps:

1. Sit in a closed circle of 6 to 10 people.

2. Reflect on some core material for a minute or so (explained in the next section). Sometimes this consists of a pithy saying or topic, seleted by the group leader, that might reasonably generate many legitimate points of view. Sometimes the focus is more practical and concrete, such as particpants' personal experiences with a strategy or concept that will be examined in the reflective study phase.

3. Anyone can begin. Each person says something of her own choosing about the subject, with a time limit of one or two minutes. People can share personal experiences or wax philosophical. After waiting a few seconds after someone has finished, the person on the left goes next. The direction of sharing continues around the circle.

4. While a person is sharing, all the other participants are silent. No jokes, interruptions, comments, agreements, or disagreements are permitted. Participants express neither opposition nor verbal support, though there can, of course, be empathy or spontaneous laughter. The role of the other participants is to pay attention and listen as fully as they can, while doing their best to suspend judgment for or against what is being said.

5. The group leader monitors timing and participation. No one needs to speak for the entire allotted time, and no one should exceed the allotted time. Ideally, everyone should say something and not just "pass."

6. If a person does pass, go back to that person (continuing to the left) after everyone else has shared. This procedure is done for two reasons. First, if a person passes, others may worry or focus on that, and that takes up mental space. And second, it is important

that everyone contribute energy to the group—the circle is not a place where some just observe others.

Material to Use

The material can vary from abstract big ideas to focused practical problems, depending on what the group wants to accomplish.

Big Ideas

For big ideas, we use what we call principles of connectedness, culled from many sources. Here are some examples:

- Everything is separate and connected.
- What is, is always in process.
- Reality consists of matter, energy, and meaning.
- Order is present everywhere.
- Inner and outer reflect each other.
- The whole is greater than the sum of the parts.
- Everything comes in layers.
- Everything is both part and whole simultaneously.
- Reality is both linear and nonlinear.
- Rhythms and cycles are present everywhere.
- Stable systems resist change; dynamic systems exist by changing.
- The whole is contained in every part.
- Order emerges out of chaos.

Principles such as these can spur initial discussion around many possible goals and issues—for example, developing an integrated curriculum. The ideas embodied in these principles are so general that they may generate many possible meanings and many personal experiences. Hence, they have no one right or wrong "answer."

Here is an example of an ordered sharing that we recorded. The core idea was "Rhythms and cycles are present everywhere."

P1: I am always fascinated by the rhythms and cycles of cities, of what becomes fashionable and not fashionable when a style of architecture is seen as exciting and new versus old versus being rediscovered again, maybe not in the same form, but there is still a celebration of those earlier styles.

P2: I thought about the origins of the universe... whether this is the first time it has expanded out or the 52nd time... we don't know, but there is a rhythm.

P3: What came to my mind was more individual cycles, starting out as young infants how we seek knowledge and practice that knowledge, we seek independence and practice that independence. And then as we get older we continue through so many years to do the same thing over and over again.

P4: I love the rhythm and the cycle of a day. We wake up very energized and refreshed and look forward to the things that come before us during that day... sometimes we're energized during the day... sometimes we have to pull ourselves up by the bootstraps again... and at certain times during the day we have moments of contemplation, and to me the day ends that way... contemplating how I can live the next day better.

Note that the individual comments are unrelated to each other, and they range from grand visions of the cosmos to how we live our lives each day. That is precisely what should happen. This range of reflections opens the minds of participants to possibilities that might not have occurred to them, and it shows that other people in the group often have ideas and perspectives that are unexpected and refreshing. It does not matter if the ideas and opinions are not directly related to the content that will be studied later. Rather, the purpose is to set the stage for being open to multiple possibilities and to listen fully to what might otherwise be missed or ignored.

Other "big idea" material can also be used for the ordered sharing. Participants may suggest a pithy saying or proverb. It is possible to use more concrete material extracted from a book, for instance, that will be the subject of the professional development program. A colleague of ours who used the ordered sharing process at the start of each meeting of his college course stretched the envelope. Rather than use words, he invited participants to reflect on and then talk about a print of a great work of art.

Practical Issues

When the focus is practical issues, the goal is simply to ask a question that invites participants to share from personal experience without feeling any obligation to "get it right" or solve the problem the group faces. Thus the process leader may say to participants, "Please share any thoughts you have or experiences you have had in dealing with discipline problems in a school [or getting students excited about math, or finding ways to connect with parents and the community]."

In the following example, the group was asked to share their ideas about and experiences with "discipline issues in a school":

P1: There was a small group in the school that disturbed everyone, and I had them in my class. I knew that I had to deal with their leader, but I got it wrong. I confronted him publicly about why he did not use his leadership to help instead of make things worse. Bad step. I should have met with him privately and asked for his help in making the lessons more useful.

P2: I worked in a small school where troublemakers were kept in after school was over. No effect. Then we got a new custodian, and after a few months there had been a major shift in the atmosphere in the school. Turns out that he began coaching soccer informally, and after that the kids went on his rounds with him and started to help clean up! Suddenly they began to get in the face of other kids who were writing graffiti and messing about—seems like they decided it was their territory and they didn't want it messed with.

P3: I once attended an inservice at a little elementary school in the mountains. There was this one teacher; I think her name was Dorris. All the other teachers thought she was fabulous. One thing that she did was to make sure that every student, even if there were 30 or more, had some personal responsibility for making something work. One kept the calendar, another handled trash, there was one who recorded attendance, and a whole lot more. She had each one of them thinking it was up to them to make things work—she almost never had a discipline problem.

P4: This is just about one student. I once volunteered at a charter high school that was filled with troubled kids. They simply refused to talk to or even look at most of us, and we couldn't do a thing with them. One day the school was preparing for a gathering of parents. A table had to be moved, and I found myself carrying it with one of the guys who had ignored me. We were near a basketball hoop and I found myself saying I had never played, and was he any good? I guess this challenged him. Anyway, he shot a hoop; then I tried and made a complete mess of it. Then he told me I should stand differently, and we kept going for about 20 minutes. After that, we could always talk freely, and I connected with a couple of his friends. I think that somehow or other I stopped being this superior alien and became more of an equal.

Again, the individual comments reflect different experiences. But two wonderful things were happening. First, the process ensured that everyone was listening to everyone else. And second, a wide range of ideas was introduced that set the stage for the discussion. In particular, it became evident that the situation could be dealt with in many different ways, and that many reasons might explain discipline problems in a school. In this situation, a theme that began to emerge, and that the group dealt with in depth in the reflective study sessions that followed, was that one key to reducing discipline problems is to improve relationships throughout the school.

The Thinking Behind the Process

Each aspect of the ordered sharing has a reason or rationale to support it. First, in terms of the seating arrangement, indigenous peoples have used circles for ages as the structure for meeting together. One reason is that a circle reduces the sense of hierarchy that usually occurs when someone is at the head of a table or the front of a room. Another is that everyone can see and be seen fully. Both factors contribute to the sense of community.

Second, participants are learning to be totally honest and to be free to express their own opinions; the freedom to choose what to share when it is their turn helps the development of this sense of freedom. At the same time, the variety exposes the other participants to some ideas, experiences, and points of view that they may not usually encounter. This exposure helps to expand what they assume to be "true" or their sense of the "right answer." We call this "expanding their cognitive horizons."

Third, full attention, silent listening, and the suspension of judgment are the hallmarks of deep listening and can only be mastered with practice. This aspect of the process could be called the development of a "beginner's mind," which refers to having an attitude of openness, eagerness, respectfulness, and a lack of preconceptions about a subject or issue or person, just as a beginner would. It develops, in part, as we listen to others nonjudgmentally. Participants will fall off the wagon time and time again, and just need to get back on. This element can be very difficult for educators and others when the practices of the culture include the right to interrupt each other, and it is, perhaps, the most challenging aspect. Over time, however, people begin to grasp the fact that everyone is treated equally and will have an opportunity to share, and that it is a delight to be able to express an authentic opinion without being concerned about a critical response.

Fourth, everybody is invited to say something because a group simply functions better when everyone contributes some energy. Some people can find it daunting to *have to* talk for a minute (or even for a couple of seconds), but ordered sharing is not a process for those who just want to observe. At the same time, in most group situations one or a few people tend to dominate, and this process creates space for everyone to be a full participant. So it sets a limit on those who are loquacious—even though they may find it frustrating to be confined to a minute.

Fifth, the reason for going back to those who passed the first time around is both to give them time to think (if needed) and to have them share in the second round so that their energy is invested in the process. There is no magic to the order of sharing. However, proceeding in one direction ensures that people do not jump in and compete for time, while also helping to build a sense of orderliness and coherence. The PrLC format provides opportunities at other times for more complex, unordered conversations.

Sometimes a participant may share something extremely personal or shocking to the rest of the group. For example, at one session a teacher started to tear up as she disclosed that her mother had died the previous day—something she had not revealed to anyone until that moment. Ordinarily, people would lean forward and express sympathy. During this process, however, all the other participants just sat and listened in respectful silence. Then the ordered sharing continued. When it was over, participants shared their deep sympathy with the teacher. In this particular case, the process leader could have pursued an alternative. The entire process could have been suspended for a while. Had that happened, then the ordered sharing would need to begin again if the participants wanted the group to continue.

Using the Ordered Sharing for Meetings and Teaching

The ordered sharing process can be adapted to many different situations, including setting the stage for meetings and teaching listening in the classroom.

Setting the Stage for Meetings

One of the people with whom we first tested the process in 1994 has become a school principal. She now uses the ordered sharing as a standalone process at the start of staff meetings. The process itself is quite explicit and understood. Even so, she (very briefly) repeats the guidelines. Then she selects a topic or an idea that seems to her to be appropriate to the meeting itself. On one occasion, for instance, she asked participants to share their thoughts about "what it means to sustain order on the playground" as a prelude to a discussion about some discipline issues that had emerged. Others have done the same, because ordered sharing is a simple and effective way to both experience and communicate the value of listening to each other so that it becomes possible to more easily deal with hard issues or see alternative possibilities.

Handling Divisive Issues

Much of the time the atmosphere in a group will be good, and so the ordered sharing just helps to make sure that everyone participates and is listened to. At other times the atmosphere may be quite fractious, perhaps because of the divisive nature of the issues under consideration, ranging from working out how to handle district requirements to dealing with issues raised by parents. In these circumstances, it is even more important to ensure that everyone is listened to—and the ordered sharing can make that easier. In fact, the ordered sharing is often a good way to help rebuild a field of listening in a staff meeting. The process leader, or a participant, can suggest that the atmosphere is getting quite heated. The leader can then frame a question to which everyone provides an answer. It may be something like this: "Things seem to be heating up. What do you feel is going on?" The point is that *everyone* has an opportunity to express an opinion and to be heard, while the principle of respectful listening is reintroduced.

Teaching Listening in the Classroom

The ordered sharing can be an effective way to help students learn to listen to each other and work together. To work in a classroom, the process calls for some preparation and some changes.

First, it might be advisable to fishbowl the process, so that students can see what to do. Here, a small group (say, three people) can engage in the process while everyone else watches and grasps how it works. Second, students will need to be organized in small groups, all of which will go through the process simultaneously (otherwise the process might consume an entire class period). It also will help for some students to be coached in how to lead the groups. Third, care must be taken to formulate the key question or core material so that it makes sense to students and elicits the sorts of responses that are sought.

The ordered sharing can be used very effectively as part of a practice of conflict resolution, or to deal with heated situations in the classroom. In these circumstances, one question might simply be this: "In your opinion, what happened?"

Some Words of Caution

Not all people like the ordered sharing process initially, and so some may express irritation, for instance, at *not* being free to interrupt. It can be very easy, in these circumstances, to dilute the process. In a word, *don't*. Often people resist change because they do not like to have patterns disrupted. In this case, the disruption, if any, is precisely what is needed, and we strongly urge you to adhere to the guidelines. Over time, and for almost everyone, the process becomes second nature and highly valued.

Another problem that sometimes occurs is the expression of opinions that others find deeply offensive. This can escalate into a complex problem and can be compounded by the deep and conflicting convictions that people often have. Much of the time the best response is no response. One key, after all, is learning to suspend judgment. However, some assertions and opinions test the limits of the process.

It may be that at the end of the ordered sharing or the group meeting the participants need to discuss their own protocols and develop some criteria that they agree to implement about what is and is not acceptable. How to proceed here requires a judgment call by the process leader or the group, to be made in the best way they know how. The keys are to bear in mind that participation is voluntary, that the group has the right to protect their own integrity, and that the process of respectful listening needs to be maintained even in the midst of impassioned discussion.

→| |← →| |← →| |← →| |←

Checklist for Ordered Sharing

1. Formulate the question.

• Review the stage in the overall process that has been reached and the purpose for the upcoming PrLC meeting.

• Decide whether the ordered sharing will be about a big idea or specific material that is being examined.

• Select the big idea or formulate a clear question about the material that will be dealt with.

2. Clarify the spirit of ordered sharing in your own mind.

• Take a moment before the meeting to remind yourself of the first goal of the ordered sharing, which is to create a field of listening.

3. Conduct the ordered sharing.

• Sit in a closed circle.

• Introduce core material and allow time for reflection.

• Anyone can begin, and each person shares in turn, to the left, around the circle.

• While a person is sharing, all the other participants are silent.

• The group leader monitors timing and participation.

• If a person passes, go back after everyone else has shared.

4. Develop critical skills, including

- Nonjudgmental listening to oneself and others
- Patience for genuine listening
- A feel for "beginner's mind"

→| |← →| |← →| |← →| |←

The PrLC at Spring Valley School

The group is together for its first meeting of the month. The topic is the idea that "the brain/mind is social." In this session the circle members are specifically exploring the social nature of learning and the ways in which individual understanding is influenced by others.

The process leader has decided that the core question will relate to the actual material being examined—in this case, the social nature of learning. The leader briefly describes the ordered sharing process. Each person will share personal thoughts. There is absolutely no need to refer to what anyone else has said, and the personal thoughts are always expressed in the first person. The leader has decided to ask participants the following question about their personal experience: "When has your knowledge or understanding about something been directly or indirectly influenced by others?" Each person shares in turn.

> *Ramona*: I remember as a kid I just could not understand how equations worked in algebra. One day I was sitting on a bench in the playground with a friend. I just vented! And then she explained equations to me, and it all made sense. The teacher had been trying for months, and my friend did it in 10 minutes! It felt totally different from working with my teacher. My friend and I were just there together and... she wasn't making a big deal about it. And she was talking like me. It just made the whole thing easier. All the stuff my teacher was saying just suddenly made sense.

Jayson: I love movies. But sometimes I only understand some of the themes when we get together after a movie, usually at our local coffeehouse, and just talk about it. We usually just talk about what we liked and did not like, but Bess really knows this stuff, and when she talks about a movie a whole new dimension opens up.

Camille: I would love to play a musical instrument, and I've had lessons sometimes. But I can't help wishing that my parents had been more musical. I know one kid. His mother studied opera and his father is a classical guitarist. He grew up just breathing music. It must be wonderful to have been immersed like that in music.

Others add their thoughts, including any who passed on their turn the first time.

6

Reflective Study

It is not hard to learn more. What is hard is to unlearn when you discover yourself wrong.

—Martin H. Fischer, physician and author

Education should be intellectually rigorous—and so should professional development. It is essential for teachers to have a deep understanding of both academic content and how individuals learn, including what great teaching calls for. Paradoxically, this requirement means that it is important to appreciate and tolerate ambiguity and confusion, because when we are confused it means that we have not made up our minds and we have not made what Ellen Langer (1989) calls "premature cognitive commitments."

Reflective study is the way to develop intellectual rigor. The purpose of this segment of the process learning circle is *not* to work out what to do on Monday morning. The purpose is to engage in a personalized and intellectual inquiry into the thinking behind any strategy or solution for a specific issue.

We apply this approach to all aspects of professional development. In our own programs with schools, we devote the entire first year to working with our brain/mind learning principles, both in theory and in practice (see Appendix A). Our reasoning is that everything that educators do should be grounded in a state-of-the-art understanding of how people learn and what good learning environments should be like. In fact, we find that the more educators have this foundation, the easier it is for them to then deal with specific issues (such as discipline) or the teaching of individual subjects (such as math).

Others may wish to begin differently, perhaps to deal immediately with an issue such as improving the climate in a school or improving the teaching of reading or math. Irrespective of the chosen focus, increasing competence calls for in-depth understanding of the issue being dealt with and, over time, of how suggested solutions relate to how students actually learn. Otherwise teachers will be acquiring a few strategies without the capacity to apply them appropriately to a wide range of students in differing contexts.

In effect, this aspect of the PrLC is setting a tone for a deep shift in the way that many educators approach their work. We suggest that *every* step that is taken or strategy that is adopted should be solidly grounded in research, and that the key to establishing an atmosphere in which students are focused on learning and understanding begins with the staff having that very attitude.

This mind-set means that the process being covered in this book is intended to apply to programs and procedures that are themselves well supported by research and experience. Sometimes mandated programs are trivial, incompatible with other mandated programs, or inadequate in other ways. Teachers and administrators who have to deal with this situation are placed in an impossible situation. Sometimes, in these circumstances, reflective study is a way to explore the dilemma and decide on a plan of action.

The Dual Aspects of Understanding

Irrespective of whether the PrLC deals with academic or professional content, the key is to integrate professional with personal learning. That is why reflective study works at two levels, each of which requires an allocation of time. First, time needs to be provided for rigorously thinking and talking about the central concepts, research, and processes with a view to understanding them. Ideally this involves both clarifying what an author is advocating, and comparing and contrasting that with what others have said. Second, time needs to be allocated to sharing personal experiences, anecdotes, and stories relevant to the material being studied. This helps to personalize it, make it real, and make it useable in the world of the classroom and the school.

The Process

Here are the core components of the reflective study phase of the PrLC.

1. Decide upon and, if necessary, distribute material ahead of time. This can be done in many different ways. Sometimes it is a decision made by school leadership, but staff can also participate. If the material is no more than a page or two, participants can read it comfortably within the time allocated in the meeting for reflective study. Usually, however, the material is lengthier—perhaps a chapter of a book, which means that the process leader needs to send materials (or references listing materials to be read or videos to be viewed) to participants several days before the meeting. Everything possible should be done to ensure that the material is read, or viewed, at least once.

2. Support and foster individual interests. One aspect of relaxed alertness as a state of mind (discussed in Chapter 1) is that it enables participants to explore topics of genuine personal interest in a way that is both rigorous and safe. The practical implication is that participants need to have time and the opportunity to ask their own questions and find their own way in which to approach the material. One way to do this is with the initial questions that are asked to launch the discussion. Here are some examples:

- What stands out for you in this material?
- What interests you?
- How does this material connect with issues and questions that you have been dealing with elsewhere?

3. Share personal stories about how the ideas or materials were experienced. The underlying question is always this: What happened to you in connection with this? For example, if the topic is about the fact that the brain/mind is social and that we all learn socially, a question might be "Recall some of the ways in which you learned in a group" or "Reflect on an occasion in which your opinion or ideas were influenced by others."

This personalization of the material can be done in at least two distinct ways:

• The PrLC can begin with an ordered sharing of personal experiences related to this material (rather than on a general principle of connectedness).

• Participants can introduce personal stories during the intellectual analysis of the material.

4. Analyze and discuss the material. The idea behind this component is to think through and examine the content. To continue our example, if you are discussing the notion that learning is social, you might discuss what "social" means, because social learning can be formal or informal, direct or indirect, with or without peers and mentors, and so on. Or, if research is supplied, you could clarify what it seeks to prove and whether the researcher ignored any issues. Or you could unpack the examples given in the readings to see what they are really illustrating.

The conversation can take place in a group of the whole, or participants can break into smaller groups. You could also alternate these modes from month to month. The key is to establish a basic routine and then to explore material in different ways. Here are some questions and processes that can add depth to the reflective study.

Analytical Questions
   • What is the primary theme or essence of … ?
   • What are the core concepts or terms?
   • How might we explain what is being said in other ways?
   • Is there a central metaphor that is being used?
   • What other writings/ideas does this most remind you of?

- How is it the same or similar? How is it different?
- What are the main assumptions?
- What is the most essential evidence for and against the main contentions?

Personal Questions
- What is most attractive or compelling to you about this?
- What is most off-putting?
- What experiences does this material call to mind?
- Do some personal journaling in which you express your own feelings and impressions.
- What type of music does this call to mind?
- Draw/diagram some aspect of the material.

Proactive Question
- What questions come to mind, emerging out of this, that are *really* interesting to you and worth pursuing?

Hints and Suggestions

The following hints and suggestions can help make the reflective study component engaging and productive for everyone involved.

Avoid just chatting. It can be extremely tempting to simply start chatting about everyday events or to focus attention on problems that crop up during the day, rather than to genuinely share personal experiences, beliefs, and assumptions related to the material in question. As much as possible, help participants avoid the temptation to "bird-walk" in unrelated directions.

Use the reflective study session to trigger additional informal discussions. Most of the time participants will find much more to explore than can be covered during the period allocated to reflective study. For that reason we invite participants to carry on their conversations on the topic in the days following the meeting. In fact, many learning circle participants have reported that they have spontaneously begun to have more in-depth conversations about learning and teaching as a natural consequence of this general process.

Consider introducing the material with a global experience. The easiest way to introduce material is with some writings. A much more powerful and effective way is for the process leader to design a short experience that is compelling and that engages emotions, senses, and memories of participants. One example might be to use a brief segment of a powerful video. Among the excellent online sources for such material are YouTube (http://www.youtube.com/), TeacherTube (http://www.teachertube.com/), and TED (http://www.ted.com/).

Use active listening. Most people tend to use a sort of personal shorthand when they express their ideas or relate anecdotes. It can be helpful to an individual and to the entire group if the process leader and participants ask occasional questions for the purpose of clarification. One approach is to use the foundational formula of active listening, which is to feed back what you think you hear—for example, "I think I heard you say such-and-such. Is that what you mean?" (for more guidance, see Caine, R., et al., 2008). Another version is to ask, "What, specifically, do you mean by such-and-such?" A third, and more intellectually rigorous, approach is to compare what a person says with something else that the person has said: "How does what you have just said relate to the point you [or someone else] made earlier about such-and-such?"

The key here is to use questions not to make a competing point but to penetrate meanings or to get at the essence of an experience. For more suggestions, you can search the web using the keywords "active listening." One helpful site is http://www.studygs.net/listening.htm.

Make sure participants have approximately equal time. This is a common issue, as some individuals can get enthusiastic and passionate over some material, and others simply tend to take over conversations. The ordered sharing approach helps to establish the atmosphere of full participation, but the idea needs to be reinforced in the reflective study aspect of the process.

One suggestion is that after someone has contributed two or three times, that person's further contribution should be discouraged until others who want to share have spoken. If this is difficult to enforce in a friendly way, invite the group to create its own guide-lines as to how to ensure that all people have adequate opportuni-ties to participate without feeling that they are competing for time.

Another suggestion is to use a talking stick—an object, such as a pen, that can be easily passed from one person to another. The rule is that only the person holding the talking stick can talk. It must be physically handed over to someone else before that other person can speak. This approach makes it possible to preserve the field of listen-ing and for the group as a whole to monitor the opportunities that participants get to speak.

A third possibility is to call for the use of the ordered-sharing format.

Important Reminder: Enjoy Not Knowing

As we suggested at the start of this chapter, one of the best states of mind to bring to the reflected study discussion is the tolerance of confusion and ambiguity. Complex ideas and skills take time to digest and master. That is why the best approach is to avoid feeling a need to understand immediately and to actually delight in knead-ing and exploring what the material being studied really means. You will see elements of the "beginner's mind" (discussed in Chapter 5) in the vignettes at the end of this and other chapters.

→| |← →| |← →| |← →| |←

Checklist for Reflective Study

1. Decide upon and, if necessary, distribute material ahead of time.

• Preparation is critical to depth of understanding and a genu-inely rigorous approach.

2. Support and foster individual interests.

• Ensure that participants have time and the opportunity to ask their own questions and find their own way in which to approach the material. This can be done with the simple question "What interests you about this?"

3. Share personal stories about how the ideas or materials were experienced.

• The question is always "What experiences have you had in connection with this?"

4. Analyze and discuss the material.

• The key is to think through and examine the content. Here are some initial ways to lead the discussion:

– "Describe how this procedure works."
– "Explain the core ideas and themes in your own words."
– "What does this remind you of?"
– "What else comes to mind?"
– "Let's look at the pros and cons."

5. Develop critical skills.

• Active listening
– Intellectual analysis
– Personalizing learning

→| |← →| |← →| |← →| |←

The PrLC at Spring Valley School

The group is together for its first meeting of the month.

1. The *ordered sharing* has been completed.

2. The group is ready to begin *reflective study*.

The leader briefly describes the reflective study component. Everyone should have read Chapter 4 of *The Brain, Education, and the Competitive Edge* (Caine, G., & Caine, R., 2001), which deals with memory, the power of context, and the social nature of learning. In addition, the process leader has prepared a short slide show on the topic "The Brain/Mind Is Social" and has distributed a few pages of additional material. The slide show is presented, and then participants scan or read the handouts. After a few minutes, the discussion begins.

Process leader: So, what are the main points of the material we're dealing with?

Melany: One key for me is the notion that there are neurons in the brain that naturally respond to others. What are they called? Oh, yes. Mirror neurons.

Process leader: Let's look at mirror neurons in a little more depth. Does the handout make sense?

The participants revisit the fact that researchers discovered mirror neurons by studying monkeys that were observing each other, and they look at the implications for learning from imitation and modeling.

Sasha: But does everybody always respond to everything?

Camille: The second handout talks about the importance of prestige. I wonder if that is why peer pressure is so important.

Dan: OK. Now I see why I've got to find a way to help them learn from each other....

Ramona: ... And that's why the things that *we* do are so important. If I'm frightened of math and never use it, no wonder the kids get scared!

The discussion continues, and then the process leader suggests a change in format.

Process leader: It looks like we have several different points here. Let's divide into groups, and each group selects one issue to look at. Then we can get back together with summaries to share.

The participants form groups. Some read and talk; others search the web for possibly relevant topics. Then the groups report back. They all realize that groups and classrooms have more of a social component than they had thought. But it's not all clear-cut. One group decided that although we all have mirror neurons, people don't always respond to others in the same way because some people are more influential than others. And another group found that the way that people respond in social settings is called "situated cognition" and that it has been translated into the notion of "communities of practice," with several practical guidelines.

The general conclusion is that the way that students in classrooms deal with academics and with standards is shaped and influenced by how their peers and the teachers deal with it all. And so it is important to start introducing social learning into classes. That's what they have to work on and experiment with.

7

Implications for Practice, Commitment to Action, and Action Research

Whatever you can do, or dream you can do, begin it. Boldness has genius, power, and magic in it.

—Attributed to Goethe

If the goal of professional development is the development of real skills, then the material being studied has to be applied in some way. It is absolutely essential to try things in real-world settings and then take the time to learn from that experience. This aspect of the PrLC process ensures that participants take action systematically and reflect on it, which requires a discussion about implications for practice, a decision to take some action, and procedures for learning adequately from the action taken. In a general sense, that is what we mean by action research.

Although action research has been explored in depth for decades, the idea is finally taking hold in the wider education community. Here, for instance, are points from several articles in a recent issue of *Educational Leadership* on "How Teachers Learn":

• The first action that teachers should take is learning about themselves. (Nieto, 2009)

• Leaders learn by "extracting lessons from performance." (Donaldson, 2009)

- There are three types of action research. First-person research is about self, second-person research is collaborative and is about issues of a group, and third-person action research deals with more global phenomena. (Brighton, 2009)
- Ongoing, job-embedded, collaborative research should replace one-day workshops. (Chappius, Chappius, & Stiggins, 2009)

In the next sections we describe how this phase of the PrLC process might unfold. Typically, at the first meeting each month, after the essential material is introduced, a small amount of time—say, 25 minutes—is allocated to deciding what to practice in the next week to 10 days. This includes discussing the implications for practice and making a formal commitment to the agreed-upon action.

Discussing Implications for Practice

Picking up on the vignette at the end of Chapter 6, let us continue to imagine that the material for a month (or a year) is focused on the social nature of learning. That, after all, is the foundation for professional learning communities. Imagine, further, that the group has had intensive discussions on the subject, perhaps going back to collaborative learning and extending forward to research that shows that the brain/mind is social and to the power of social networking.

Now is the time to discuss the implications for practice. In general terms, such a discussion will likely revolve around the idea that teaching can be enhanced, and some discipline problems reduced, if ways are found to help students learn with and from each other. The challenge, then, is to select an aspect of the social nature of learning to put into practice in the next few weeks.

Making a Commitment to Action

The objective is simply for each participant to make a commitment to trying something out, based upon what transpired in the reflective study and the discussion about implications for practice. Participants can work alone or together as they decide what to focus on and write it down. Then each publicly shares with the entire group the commitment that has been made.

Here are some examples of the kinds of actions that individuals might decide to take:

- Use the ordered sharing process on a regular basis in the classroom.
- Research collaborative learning and map out a program for students for a full semester or more.
- Use group projects for the first time.
- Give every student some kind of leadership function in the class every week.
- Help students learn how to listen and how to resolve conflicts.
- Introduce the concept of learning or identity styles to students so that they can better understand how they are like and unlike other students, and why there can be such differences in how they all function together.

The particular actions that are adopted should reflect, and will be guided by, the materials that the circle members used in the reflective study.

Action Research

Traditionally, action research has more depth and is more systematic than the process we are advocating here. Indeed, much of the time practitioners use some quite substantial research protocols.

The process described in this book is not quite as rigorous because it assumes that teachers are still learning what to deal with and how to assess results. It is therefore important to allow the procedure to unfold rather than to feel enormous pressure to generate better results immediately. Over time, as the process is refined and alternatives are examined, teachers will gain a deeper understanding and better feel for what they are working on, and their skill (and results) will improve. One example is the experience of the teacher described in Chapter 2 who focused on learning to tell stories. She even solicited feedback from her students about what they liked and did not like about the way she told stories.

Another example is the way that a teacher named Brett first thought about authentic assessment in his 7th grade class. He was initially overwhelmed by all the possibilities. And he knew that he did not use the sort of complex projects that form the basis of portfolios. So he decided that for a short period every afternoon he would ask his students (one at a time) to sit with him at his desk and tell him what seemed to be working and what they were struggling with. He was astounded at how honest and direct they were, and at what he was finding out—about them, the materials he was using, the social happenings in the classroom, and what his students really cared about. What started as an almost lip-service approach to something became just the first step in his own multiyear learning journey from "talk and drill" to quite sophisticated project-based learning.

During the experimental efforts for the two weeks after the PrLC meeting, a teacher needs to make observations and take notes—to the extent possible. The sheer demands of teaching mean that most notes will be made after a class is over. The challenge is to observe and recollect what happened in as much detail as possible. Here are some questions to consider:

• What seemed to appeal to students? What did not? How could you tell?

• What helped their focus and attention? What did not? What is your evidence either way?

• What seemed to work better after several attempts?

• What was the best and most natural fit for you as the teacher?

• What student behaviors were the best indicators of the concepts being tested (e.g., that learning is social)?

Working with a Critical Friend

Many, many questions could be asked, and the process can be easy or rigorous. The great challenge is to be honest, and a major problem is that people see things through their own eyes and so may miss some of what is going on.

One solution is to team up with a colleague so that each helps the other. You can take turns observing each other's practice. Then, in private, provide honest feedback. This can also be the role of an administrator or some other professional with expertise in a particular area such as reading. Our experience is that supporting the practical implementation of ideas and procedures is one of the great contributions that school leadership can provide. However, it is vital to maintain the sense of safety and growth so that feedback helps and does not hurt. So choose the critical friend carefully. Ideally, it should be a person who either knows the PrLC process or who has a similar philosophy.

Observing Others

One of the best ways to become more proficient at anything is to observe, talk to, and be with others who are more competent than we are. So part of the action can include observing other teachers and talking with them about what they do and how they think about it. This is much more useful than feeling some sort of obligation to "go it alone."

Learning Circle Follow-up:
The Second Meeting of the Month

About two weeks after the first learning circle meeting, participants gather again. This follow-up is the key to making practice and action research effective. The purpose is for participants to spend most of the time sharing and discussing, analyzing and reflecting on their experience, on how students reacted, and on the evidence gathered. Sharing with others will help to clarify memories and strengthen understanding. And each will benefit a great deal from the insights that others have and from the questions that they might ask. Initially this can be done relatively informally, but over time it becomes an excellent opportunity for more systematic data analysis.

It is essential to retain the central phases of the PrLC, but they are all reframed a little because they all focus on the action taken over the preceding two weeks. The following sections explain the process in more detail.

Phase 1: Ordered Sharing

This phase now has two clear purposes. The original purpose of initiating (and sustaining) a field of listening continues. In addition, this is also the time for participants to share with each other by recounting what they practiced and experimented with and how they fared. This segment should be brief because the group will have more time for reflection later. Note that this is *not* a time for interruptions or questioning by others. So the initial questions from the process leader might take this form:

- What did you work on and observe during the last two weeks?
- What insights did you come to?
- What still puzzles you?

Phase 2: Reflective Study

This phase allows for a much longer, open-ended conversation than the ordered sharing. It is the time when participants have a substantial opportunity to talk through their experiences, introduce any evidence or data that they collected, and think more deeply about what happened. Because everyone will need to reflect and talk, it may be appropriate to divide into pairs or groups of three so that enough time is available for everything that needs to be done. During this phase, participants use active listening to ask each other questions, or they can ask for advice and suggestions. This phase can also be used to introduce additional intellectually challenging material, or to revisit the material examined in the first meeting now that it has been tried and tested a little. For instance, a person might share as follows:

I tried one aspect of active listening with my students and my colleagues. It felt a little strange, but there were some noticeable differences in how some of them responded to me. I want to continue, but I think I need to increase my range of questioning skills quite a lot.

Phase 3: Implications for Practice

On the basis of what they learn and feel as a result of proceedings so far, participants can now take some time to think through how best to proceed for the next two weeks. They may decide to do more of the same, or they may decide to vary what they have been trying out in the classroom. Either way, they express a renewed commitment to action, with the intention of learning from the action.

Phase 4: Regrouping

The regrouping phase remains the same. Participants take the opportunity to consolidate what they are learning about the new ideas and practices that they are exploring, though they may also begin to notice other aspects of their practice that they had not noticed before (a possibility that we explore in Chapter 8). The regrouping is done in the form of a final ordered sharing.

Quality Control

Learning enough from experience involves two major challenges. The first is to have the right sort of experience. The second is to process that experience adequately—to see and hear and feel and think enough about what actually happened in order to fully benefit.

Sometimes the very practices that are powerful in some ways and are most frequently recommended for professional development actually get in the way because they don't meet these criteria. One example is peer coaching. It is really helpful to go through this process by working with colleagues and friends. Just having some support makes a big difference. And the opportunity to talk things through with friends and colleagues is often a delight as well as a source of understanding and insight. However, sometimes our peers do not know any more than we do. Sometimes a peer will give advice based on what she thinks, and that advice will be inadequate.

All the research on the development of expertise shows that having coaches or mentors who are already competent is useful and important. We need to see things being done the right way, and we need to get feedback from people who can already do what we are learning how to do.

Those criteria make it essential to select someone who can provide high-level feedback. If that person is a good coach, she can help us see things that we might not have seen, catch critical moments that might otherwise have escaped us, and put things together so that we get a better idea of how different practices can work.

In our work with schools, one of the key components is to ensure that team members visit classrooms regularly in order to provide educative feedback to teachers using the process. Another way to expand the range of support available is to start searching the web for sites and blogs and groups of people to talk to. Although the range of opinions is vast, we have found invaluable support by going online.

Tips and Suggestions

The following tips and suggestions can help make the action research phase of the PrLC more effective.

Keep a journal. Journaling is an effective reflective tool that works on several levels. You can use it to keep a running record of what you have attempted and what the results were. You can also use it in a more personal way to recount your own feelings and reactions—about both the specific events being tested and more general concerns. Journaling helps you make the connections between what you have learned and felt and accomplished in the past, and it helps to more fully integrate the actual concepts, strategies, and processes you are exploring. Note that many technologies are now available to effectively help teachers keep a sort of collective journal. This can be done, for instance, by developing groups on social networking sites such as Facebook and Yahoo, or by using a wiki (a tool for accumulating collective expertise) (Ferriter, 2009).

Use scaffolding. We all know that students have different developmental levels and that good teaching calls for working with them at an appropriate degree of difficulty. The same point can be made about every adult. Good action research has a sort of Goldilocks quality—the project should be neither too easy nor too difficult. The problem is that quality of performance is sometimes confused with degree of difficulty. It is usually advisable to aim lower than might seem appropriate and to work for a high standard of competence. For instance, a person may just have decided to spend more time using social networking to work with colleagues, and to create a page on Facebook. Some people dive in easily and understand "fans" and "groups" and their "wall" and other aspects of Facebook. Others might simply like to take the time to work out the difference between communicating with just one person or everyone on Facebook.

Alternate between a clear and a fuzzy focus. Sometimes it is important to ask really precise questions and to be very clear about what you are experimenting with. And sometimes you don't know what a practice is all about until you just dive in and try something. That means that occasionally it is OK to just attempt a new strategy without trying to be too precise. The very fact of doing it will show you student interactions or possibilities that you have not seen before, and that can help to make everything clearer.

→| |← →| |← →| |← →| |←

Checklist for Action Research

First Monthly Meeting

1. Briefly explain or describe the concept or procedure that you want to research.

2. Briefly describe the steps that you plan to take.

3. List at least three indicators of changed behavior to look for.

4. Identify at least one other person to work with you as a process partner.

5. Create a journal in a three-ring binder for reflections, notes, and recording observations from time to time.

After the Meeting

Act on your plan and make notes of your results during the two weeks after the meeting.

6. Within two days before the second monthly meeting, create notes on what you want to talk about and, if necessary, what areas you need help with.

Second Monthly Meeting

By the end of the second monthly meeting, review and clarify or expand each of the items in your checklist.

After the Second Meeting

Act on your plan and make notes on your results during the two weeks after the meeting.

Develop critical skills, including

- A systematic approach to practice
- Action research
- Peer coaching

→| |← →| |← →| |← →| |←

The PrLC at Spring Valley School

The group is together for its first meeting of the month.

1. The *ordered sharing* has been completed.
2. The *reflective study* has been completed.
3. **The group is ready to discuss *implications for practice* and *commitment to action*.**

The participants engage in a general discussion about the implications. The general consensus is that it is sometimes easier for students to talk with friends than to talk directly to a teacher or in front of the whole class. The group also agrees that students can learn a lot from their classmates and from teacher modeling. They realize that when students are talking with each other, they can end up discussing stuff that is totally unrelated to what the class is addressing. And it is pretty clear that friends may have good ideas, but they may also have bad ones and may not necessarily teach each other. So the teacher's ongoing role is very important.

The process leader then calls for a commitment to action. Each participant reflects, individually or with others, on some personally manageable action step to take that reflects an understanding of what has been discussed. The objective is getting students to work and learn together in some way.

> *Camille*: I think I might try to rearrange the desks in my room. I'm going to see what happens when they're sitting in groups and not in rows.

> *Jayson*: I wonder what would happen if they worked on an assignment together. I think I'll let them choose partners for the next assignment and see what happens. What do you guys think?

> *Sasha*: I liked what Ramona said about learning about equations from a friend. I'd like to set up a mentoring system for my class. I've got a couple of kids who are really struggling, and I just didn't think that maybe their friends could help them out.

Note that the participants are at different stages in their instructional sophistication, and that their actions are not structured very systematically. The key is to take some action and then to learn from it. As they become clearer about the operations of the process learning circles, their own actions will become more deeply thought out and systematically designed. Using the checklist from the chapter, the process leader encourages each participant to write down what she plans to do and to prepare to observe and make notes about what happens when the planned actions take place.

8

Regrouping

The real voyage of discovery consists not in seeking new landscapes, but in having new eyes.

—Marcel Proust

We now turn to the final phase of the PrLC, which we call "regrouping." The word *regroup* has many synonyms, including *assemble, bring together, collect, gather, marshal, mobilize,* and *reassemble.* In essence, the fourth phase of the PrLC format is a time to pull together some essential learnings from the entire process, both personally and collectively. This segment is a continuation of the reflective practice that we introduced under the notion of active processing in Chapter 1.

The initial purpose, then, is to take a little time to extract additional insight and understanding from the PrLC meeting. In addition, regrouping eventually begins to occur at other times and generally takes on a life of its own as participants enjoy the experience, grasp its value, and take advantage of more and more opportunities to learn from their own work.

The Regrouping Procedure

The procedure is outwardly simple and can be outlined as follows:

• All participants are given a few minutes to reflect on the group session or the ongoing process.

• They use a seed thought supplied by the process leader, such as "What stands out for you as being most important for you from this session?"

• If time allows, people can share reflections in a collective discussion.

• Each person then briefly sums up his most important learning, using the ordered sharing process.

Regrouping Content

Regrouping can operate at two different levels, with the focus on (1) the substance of the material that the participants have been studying or (2) the skills and capacities they are developing.

In the first case, regrouping is an opportunity to pull together some core aspect of the material—a concept, an idea, a novel thought, or a relevant skill—and to clarify what it is that they will be setting out to test and experiment with in the next few weeks. The process leader usually seeds this discussion with a few questions. The questions can be general, they can be pointed, they can refer back to the intellectual content of the material, or they can call for more personalized responses about the material. Here are some examples:

• What, to you, was the gist or essence of what we dealt with in the PrLC today?

• What ideas or practices stood out? What made them stand out?

• Did this material seem to confirm or conflict with other material or ideas or practices that you have dealt with in the past? If so, in what ways?

• Did the material appeal to you? Why or why not? Did it trouble you? For what reason?

• Are there any additional experiences in your life that the material brought to mind?

In the second option, regrouping focuses on processing the lessons that the group experience offered about skills and capacities. Remember that the group process itself is teaching participants certain skills, so they can take advantage of the regrouping session to gain deeper insights. This possibility becomes evident when we look at other sorts of questions that a process leader might ask or that a participant might choose to deal with, such as the following:

Listening
- What did you discover today about listening generally?
- Did you gain any insight into how you listen?
- How important is it for people to feel heard?
- Is real listening easy? If not, what makes listening difficult?

Community
- What is the atmosphere like in our group?
- What seems to you to be most important to creating authentic community?
- What gets in the way of authentic community?
- What are your strengths and weaknesses when it comes to creating authentic community?

Understanding
- How easy is it for you to find personal examples that apply to what you are studying?
- How valuable are your stories, and the personal stories of others, to you?
- Can you see applications for this in your work?

Practice
- What are you discovering about learning by trying things out and learning without trying things out?
- Is there any difference between testing some strategy just once and testing it several times?
- What have you grasped about the developmental nature of learning?

• How might you apply any of these insights to other aspects of your work?

Other Issues

• Was there a time during the meeting when we struggled with a decision, individually or collectively? What does that tell us about us (or what does it tell you about yourself)?

• How did we respond to the way that time was used (i.e., did the meeting feel fast or slow)? What did that show about our own approach to time? For example, were there any insights to be gained about patience?

• How well did we focus on the purpose of the meeting? To the extent that we veered off course, what pulled us, and what can we learn from that?

Regrouping

• What to you are the main benefits of reflecting and regrouping?

• Which processes seem to work best for you?

• What other aspects of your work and life experience might benefit from regrouping?

Hints and Suggestions

At first regrouping may seem to be a very quick and simple process. Here are some ways to add depth, richness, and value.

Listen to each other. The ways in which we listen to each other are always critical. Even though the meeting is coming to an end, listen to each other and honor the individual lessons that participants have. When others really listen to us, we tend to take our own learning and contributions more seriously.

Adopt a relaxed and open attitude. The attitude we bring to the process contributes enormously to its value. This is not a time to rush. Rather, the key is to be in a relaxed and open mode so that you allow insights to come to mind and feel them as well as think them. That means that it is important not to pressure yourself to discover some profound and complex insight. Rather, take a moment to notice how you feel and what seems to have been most important or made an impact, and just share about that honestly. As the process becomes more comfortable, it will naturally go deeper, and so insights will begin to emerge.

Be specific. Whether reflecting on an aspect of content or on some personal characteristic, it helps to focus on a few specifics. For instance, it is easy to say that "I seem to move in and out when I listen." It is more useful to say that "I paid a lot of attention during the ordered sharing, but I found it difficult to fully listen to what others were saying during the reflective study. I think that shows that I like personal stories but don't really see much value in academic theory." This kind of comment offers an opportunity for further reflection that can lead to action. For instance, the participant might continue: "I need to look at why I feel that way about theoretical stuff. After all, that's all too often how I teach!"

Use verbal and nonverbal processes. Nonverbal processes can be effective because they help participants to see things in a different light. One technique is to draw and diagram what comes to mind by using simple flow charts. Let's apply this to listening. A participant might say, "I can see why there is much more energy when everyone is listening and there are no side conversations." She could also pull out a sheet of paper and, perhaps, draw the difference, saying something like this: "When we're all focused together it feels like this [drawing a circle of arrows with all the arrows facing in, each drawn as a firm straight line], but when there are side conversations, the energy is all over the place [drawing a bunch of arrows, some light, some dark, some dotted, with some pointing into the circle, some pointing away, and some just pointing at each other]."

This approach can seem simple and childlike. So much the better. The art of genuinely learning from experience is not to just get an intellectual idea, but to fully embody the insight—to get it in your "feelings." For that to happen, sometimes the processing needs to be done indirectly and "sideways." Using art, music, and movement are superb ways of working at this deeper level.

Realize that it's not over when it's over. Feel free to continue these conversations and discussions at other times and places. Talking and learning about ourselves is often as interesting as it is useful. And the more we actively engage in our own learning as a matter of course, the more we create an atmosphere and culture of learning in the school or organization generally.

Regrouping can be an enormously valuable life habit. Every one of us has a day's worth of experience every day, in the classroom, the staff room, online, working on projects, and in other situations. One way to add value to all that experience is to intentionally learn from it. This can be done formally (as in the process described here) or informally, while chatting over a cup of coffee. And it can be done with students as well, as they learn to reflect on their own actions and decisions, and those of their friends and others.

Finding Center

> *This above all: to thine own self be true,*
> *And it must follow, as the night the day,*
> *Thou canst not then be false to any man.*
>
> —William Shakespeare, Hamlet, Act 1, Scene 3, 78–80

Sometimes education imposes an unwelcome burden on educators. They need to choose between what they feel obliged to do and what they think is best to do. In our opinion, a key to peace of mind, and to being a respected and effective leader, is to know our own truth and to act with that truth in mind. This is sometimes called "being centered."

Being centered is enormously important for a teacher in a classroom and for an administrator at every level. It is critical in dealing with the turbulence of conflicting demands and pressures. The way to get there is to practice, and a wonderful way to start is by means of regrouping.

This is not the place to discuss in depth what it means to be centered, but many resources are available. One place to begin is

The Happiness Project (http://www.happiness-project.com/happiness _project/), which is both a book and a website in which author Gretchen Rubin shares her own happiness experiments. Her approach is light, easy, and useful. Another possibility is to research such topics as "inner leadership" and "servant leadership," with a view to clarifying what is being called for and setting up a path of practice.

Insights will begin to emerge at other times as well, and in other places, and this is the way in which deeper learning becomes a constant—and delightful—companion.

→| |← →| |← →| |← →| |←

Checklist for Regrouping

This is a time to pull together some essential learnings from the entire process. It can focus on content, or on personal and collective skills and capacities.

Core procedure
- Take a few minutes to reflect on the group session or the larger ongoing process.
  - Use a seed thought supplied by the process leader.
  - If there is time, collectively discuss the seed thought.
  - Summarize individually, using ordered sharing.

Regrouping content
The questions can be general, pointed, refer to the intellectual content of the material, or call for personalized responses to the material.

Regrouping performance and personal capacity
The skills and capacities necessary to practice regrouping are related to listening, building community, understanding, using real-world practices, and reflecting and regrouping (itself).

Hints and suggestions

- Listen to each other.
- Relax and stay open to allow insights to come to mind and to be felt.
- Be specific.
- Use verbal and nonverbal processes.
- Feel free to continue these conversations and discussions at other times and places.

Finding center

Being centered is important for teachers and administrators. A key is to know one's own truth and to act with that truth in mind. The way to get there is to practice. Regrouping is a wonderful way to begin.

Develop critical skills, including

- Active processing of experience
- Sharing with others
- Learning together

→| |← →| |← →| |← →| |←

The PrLC at Spring Valley School

The group is together for the first meeting of the month.

1. The *ordered sharing* has been completed.

2. The *reflective study* has been completed.

3. *Implications for practice and commitment to action* have been completed.

4. The group is ready for the *regrouping* phase.

For the final 10 or so minutes of the circle meeting, participants reflect on the intellectual content that they have covered or on what they learned from the group process itself about such issues as their own listening skills.

Process leader: So, what stood out for you as the main thing you learned from the meeting today?

Sasha: I'm really taken with the idea of mirror neurons, and I want to find out more.

Dore: I think the key for me was to really get the fact that kids teach each other, and that the overall climate and connections in the classroom play a big role in how they learn and what they end up understanding. This is a big shift for me. I think I'll be looking at it for a long time.

Ramona: We worked pretty well as a group today. I noticed that there were no interruptions in the ordered sharing, and we were pretty much focused when we were looking at social learning. I think it helps to have some agreements about how we all talk to each other and listen to each other. I can't wait to try to do more of this with my kids.

Jayson: Well, I discovered something about how I learn, which I need to look at. I've always thought that I picked up new stuff very quickly, and I do. But when we were doing the commitment to action today, I finally got how important it is to try things out—often—in order to be able to actually do it. The difference between understanding something and being able to do it is *huge*! I have to get much more systematic about the action research part.

Camille: I had a lot of fun today. I like being with people. It's part of my upbringing. And it was so cool to see research that shows that relationships matter, because that's what I try to do in my classroom and what I really want at work. But I can see that other people are different and that sometimes I may get too close too quickly. That happened today when Sasha and I were working together. We're very different. So I want to learn a lot more about how people are different and how to connect with people who are so... so... rational!

[Laughter]

Note the range of responses. This is an opportunity for personal learning. However, just by listening to each other, everyone gains additional insight, and many of the core lessons of the process are reinforced.

Now let's look at an example of regrouping and what can happen if the process hits a slight bump in the road.

Ramona: I am definitely going to try out the ordered sharing with the class. I am also going to Google some ideas on how to improve listening on my part so that I am a better model.

Max: I am still overwhelmed by the power of the mirror neurons and how my actions affect others and not just my words. I want to study this more. Anyone else for joining me in continuing this instead of going on in the book?

[The group launches into discussion.]

Process leader: Folks, let's do a quick process check. We need to finish our regrouping, and this *is* an ordered sharing. When this phase is over and everyone has had a chance to share, those of us who are interested can take the time to deal with Max's question.

Max: That makes sense. Let's stick with the process. I'm just finding myself really curious about my own behavior and how it has been affected by the mirror neurons as well as how I affect others.

[The sharing continues.]

The process leader takes a moment to check on details about the time and place of the next meeting and reiterates that most of the time will be spent on regrouping the actions to which they have committed.

(Note: The second meeting of the month follows the same format but has a different emphasis. An account of that meeting appears in Appendix C.)

9

The Process Leader

The challenge for leaders is to live up to their fundamental responsibility as human beings: to treat others as themselves.

—*Keshavan Nair,*
A Higher Standard of Leadership: Lessons from the Life of Gandhi

Our broad definition of a process leader is someone who creates the conditions that allow others to succeed. More specifically, process leaders are the people who guide, support, nurture, and facilitate the PrLCs. Here we dip into the role of leadership and facilitation generally, but with an emphasis on a core group of skills and capacities that help make the process effective.

Note that the process leader is not a boss, despite facilitating the learning of others. The participants in process learning circles are usually volunteers who want to be there and to benefit from the experience. So during the discussion of the process and clarifications of purpose and procedures, the issue of joint responsibility for maintaining the process should be raised, and participants should be asked if they are willing to commit to it. The implication, which can also be publicly acknowledged, is that each person supports the process. The point is that everyone is learning together—some are learning to lead; others are learning to follow and support. And all participants will have both experiences.

The art of facilitating PrLCs is to guide and to be accepted and respected as a guide, but without being the center of attention. That is why the groups should be led by good process leaders in the early stages. However, the absence of skilled process leaders should not be a bar to starting. To a large extent, the process described in this book is one of self-teaching. People begin with the skills that they have and then learn together as they go along.

Hints for First-Time PrLC Leaders

In the early stages of facilitating a PrLC, the key is to become familiar with the basics and to remind participants of those basics. We assume at this point that you have attended to issues introduced in Chapter 4 on logistics, such as gathering volunteers and deciding upon an initial venue. Here are some additional suggestions:

• Communicate logistical information to participants ahead of time. Even if they once agreed upon a time and a venue, remind them of it. And send or remind them of any preliminary material they need to read or work on. We suggest, in addition, that each participant have a copy of this book to refer to, mark up, and use.

• When people first get together, they likely will want to chat and vent. Allow a few minutes for this to happen, and then call for the attention of the group.

• In the first few meetings, follow the procedures presented in this book fairly strictly. Doing so helps develop a sense of the routine and flow. It provides a set of rails to run on. And it lays the foundation for really benefiting from the process.

• In those early meetings, reiterate the overall format. State that the process has four phases and that each has a different purpose—but keep this statement brief.

• At the beginning of each phase, be clear about what is going to happen. For instance, before the ordered sharing, repeat the steps that will be involved. And before the reflective study, state clearly that participants will be examining the material *and* recollecting stories and anecdotes from personal experience that relate to the material.

• Be moderately firm about timing. It is important to allow some flexibility, but it is absolutely essential to include enough time for all four phases of the process. After a couple of meetings, in fact, the group might voluntarily decide to extend the length of each meeting to ensure that enough time is available. It is also quite appropriate for the process leader to run a half-day or full-day workshop using all four phases of the process, but with each given substantially more time.

Important Process Skills and Capacities

Use the opportunities of being a process leader to develop a core set of skills and the inner capacities that are at the core of great leadership. These help the PrLCs function at greater and greater depth. They are also essential skills for any administrators or teachers to use in other aspects of their work.

A Capacity to Listen

People can listen in different ways and at varying depths (see Appendix B). Here are some aspects of listening to consider:

- Basic listening is part of general courtesy.
- Listening for key ideas is essential for understanding the intellectual content of any discussion.
- The art of listening includes paying attention to the social and interpersonal relationships that are playing out in the group.
- A type of deep listening develops through the practices described in this book as participants begin to grasp other people's often invisible assumptions and mental models.
- Ultimately, the capacity for listening develops into being able to listen more deeply to oneself. (We discussed this in Chapter 8 on regrouping.)

The Ability to Ask Good Questions

Sometimes it is important to clarify what people mean and what is intended, and it may require skillful questioning to elicit the meanings behind the overt behaviors. That is why part of active listening includes such skills as the art of reflecting back what we think we heard in order to make sure that we "get" it. (See Appendix B on active listening.)

Good Personal Boundaries

When things get tense or personal or difficult, as they will from time to time, it is really important for a process leader to stay centered and not take things personally. This can be difficult, especially if the process leader is blamed for the problems. A good process leader can separate the personal from the professional and deal with situations as they arise. Doing so may involve acknowledging responsibility for what has transpired. It may also involve the art of nudging people to keep the process moving, even when participants are emotionally involved.

A Center of Truth and Integrity

It can be enormously tempting to try to please others and make them happy. And it can be equally tempting to try to reshape the process in order to "produce results more quickly" or focus more directly on ultimate goals. Effective process leaders need to exercise a degree of self-discipline to avoid succumbing to those temptations.

It is not possible to please everyone. And some who are pleased at one moment can be upset at another. Although there are many different sorts of group processes, ignoring, avoiding, or overemphasizing any of the phases of the PrLCs will distort the process and almost certainly weaken it. And because the majority of participants focus primarily on their immediate needs, they tend not to have a sense of the long term and the fact that community deepens and student learning improves over time and not immediately. Combine all of these factors with the personal pressures to which leaders can be exposed, and it becomes easy to vacillate and shift in the breeze. Doing so is a recipe for failure.

Process leaders need to be able to honor their own beliefs and to have or acquire the strength to "hold their center." This is a personal challenge. It can be quite daunting. And it can be an inspiring and deeply appreciated gift to colleagues and students in the long run.

Discernment

For better or for worse, people and groups operate in layers, some of which are invisible. That means that it is not always clear what is happening, nor is it always clear what people mean or what we mean. Confusion can prevail in many ways, including the following:

• Sometimes we do not really know ourselves, even though we think we do.

• People may have something on their minds that unconsciously shapes what they say.

• Tensions or connections between individuals—or tension in the air in general—may affect what happens.

• People may have differing agendas or reasons for being in the group.

• Some participants may have and exert power to influence the direction of the group.

• Some individuals may keep going on "birdwalks" (telling unrelated stories or venturing into peripheral issues), continually sidetracking the group.

The good news and the bad news is that these sorts of issues are present in every group. They are just part of the underlying dynamic that needs to be dealt with. The processes and protocols that you find here will help with many of these. Other tools are also available to process leaders and participants, such as process checks and assumption checks, introduced in Chapter 13.

Additional Suggestions

The process leader's role is to create the conditions so that the participants begin to explore their own ideas and experiences in depth. With that end in mind, here are some additional suggestions:

- Do not preach and, most of the time, do not teach didactically. No matter how much you understand, your job is to create the conditions that allow participants, individually and collectively, to come to their own understanding about materials in question. This may require some additional training in such procedures as conflict resolution and active listening (see, e.g., Caine, R., et al., 2008). And, as the process leader, you need to remember that you are a model for the group.

- Some people will tend to dominate, and others will tend to remain silent. The goal is to avoid both extremes. More equal distribution of time tends to occur after several experiences of the ordered sharing. However, it is appropriate to specifically ask anyone who has not participated to share on occasion and to explain why. It is also appropriate to say (gently but directly) to someone who talks a lot that you will wait until everyone else has spoken before calling on that person again.

- Much of the time participants will look at you when they are talking, whereas the goal is to have them talk to and look at each other. One solution is to look away or look down when they focus too much on you. They almost always will turn and look at someone else.

- A primary function of the process leader will be to occasionally ask questions of participants (but *not* during or after the ordered sharing). These are usually questions of clarification or expansion. For instance, "I think I heard you say such and such. Is that accurate?" or "Would you elaborate on that a little?"

Leadership Development

The PrLC format is a superb vehicle for developing some aspects of leadership generally. One way to accomplish this is to rotate the role of process leader. Allow the circle to meet a few times before beginning the rotation, and then provide the opportunity to people who volunteer. Those people will need to do the work and follow the protocols. For some, leading this process will be quite a stretch. For others, especially those who tend to be leaders, being a follower will be quite a stretch. Both lessons are invaluable.

If a novice leader wants some support or guidance, feel free to offer it and be a mentor, but it is really important to allow that person to make decisions and most tough calls. When someone does lead the process for the first time, be sure to take some time after the circle meeting is over to regroup and debrief the experience so that the person can learn enough from what happened. Use similar sorts of questions to those introduced in Chapter 8 on regrouping.

Regroup Yourself

It is easy to get so caught up in doing a good job and ensuring that all details are attended to that you miss the personal learning. So it is important for process leaders to take some time after each group meeting to review what transpired and to learn from it. Some of the learning is about the process generally, and some is about your own strengths, weaknesses, and predispositions. This can also become a time to explore your values and ideas about leadership, such as "servant leadership" (Greenleaf, Spears, & Vaill, 1998). A little journaling at this time can be useful in the moment and can provide some valuable material for reflection when looking back. Sometimes it can be valuable to have a process partner, so that the two of you can help each other learn. Remember, however, that the goal is to help each other learn from your respective experiences.

On-Site Coaching and Mentoring

When implementing programs and materials to aid instruction, it is valuable to staff to have at least one person available—either on site or as a visitor—who understands and is already competent. That person can model, coach, and mentor others as they try things out. Time and time again we have noticed how much it benefits a teacher to have someone else who can provide encouragement and support, act as a friendly ear to talk things through, provide some guidance, and generally help the process along.

The on-site coach need not be the person leading the PrLC. However, it should be a person who participates in and is committed to the process, as well as being a good teacher. We discuss our view of good teaching in Chapter 15.

Our first experience with this was at Dry Creek School in the 1990s. The principal, Cindy Tucker, was enthusiastic about our principles and process, and she constantly helped teachers to see what seemed to be working and to clarify what needed additional effort. She would visit classrooms, chat with teachers privately, encourage informal conversations at different times and places, and generally help to carry the process. But other teachers actually led the PrLCs. At another school, Redwood Elementary (described in more depth in Chapter 11), Renate and a deputy principal, Janice, acted in this role. In these cases and elsewhere, the enthusiastic and competent presence of process leadership contributed immensely to the willingness of teachers to persevere, and to their capacity to think things through and learn from their experiences.

A Broader View of Leadership

Great leadership is indispensable to success in creating schools for the knowledge age. But leadership does not reside only in those with the title of principal or lead teacher. There is a way of being a participant leader—committing to a process, taking charge of your own learning, supporting the learning of others, and contributing actively to creating a culture of learning and a field of listening.

We invite, encourage, and relish the development of PrLC participants as process leaders, in part because some of the qualities and capacities they develop as leaders are precisely the qualities and capacities that are needed in great teachers. Listening and doing one's own learning matter just as much to students as they do to colleagues. For that reason, we hope it is clear that the processes being implemented in the PrLCs are as important to professional develop-ment as the specific skills and materials that each PrLC explores.

→| |← →| |← →| |← →| |←

The PrLC at Spring Valley School

1. The *ordered sharing* has been completed.
2. The *reflective study* has been completed.
3. *Implications for practice and commitment to action* have been completed.
4. *Regrouping* of the participants has been completed.

Now it is time for the process leader to regroup, using a personal journal.

Friday

The group went well today—the smoothest it's been so far. I knew it would take time for everyone to get settled, but it is really pleasing to see it happening. The ordered sharing is pretty impor-tant—when they do that right the other parts of the process seem to work better. And they're getting the hang of doing some research and thinking seriously about stuff.

I'm still a little concerned about their glibness sometimes. I'm not sure that Sasha and a couple of the others are putting in as much effort as they say they are putting in. I need to see some real changes before I can be sure. I think that I can do something about that dur-ing the meetings. I've been very supportive when they share, but I think that I need to be a bit firmer with my questions—it would be quite easy (but could be a bit tense) for me to ask Sasha to be a little more specific about what steps he plans to take, and how he would know whether he had been successful. Not sure how to do that, but I need to find a way to ask harder-nosed questions at the next meeting.

I wonder if it's time for some of the others to start leading indi-vidual sessions. I trust myself much more than any of them. That's something to think about! Maybe I've got to work a bit more on letting go.

Still, I'm pleased with the way things are going. Onward and upward!

10

Asking the Right Question

A journey of a thousand miles begins with a single step.

—Anonymous

Selecting the question to ask or the issue to focus on is one of the most important steps for school improvement and professional development. At the heart of the situation is the fact that educators (and the general public) disagree strongly and passionately about what good teaching looks like and what the conditions are for powerful learning. That disagreement spills over into every other issue that schools are called upon to address.

For example, imagine that the question being posed by the staff is "How to address discipline problems in classrooms." One research finding is that the more engaged, interested, and challenged students are in any subject area, the less likely they are to be involved in disciplinary procedures (see, e.g., the results of Learning to Learn, the large-scale reform effort in South Australia; Department of Education and Children's Services [DECS], 2004). Thus what appears to be a problem of student behavior may actually reflect an issue of teaching skill and competence, school climate, and the ability of teachers to tap into student interests and teach for meaning and understanding.

The point is that a school is a system. Everything is connected to everything else. So although it is appropriate to identify single issues that need to be addressed, the more we grasp the interconnectedness of issues, the more value we can extract from any particular course of action.

A Philosophy of Change

Leaders need a philosophy of change. In the following sections we present an overview of our approach.

Recognize That Some Things Are Off the Table

More often than ever before, teachers and schools are being directed to standardize instruction. Their districts are telling them to implement programs that prescribe in extensive detail precisely what teachers should be doing and how they should function in the classroom. Sometimes districts issue general pacing guides, so that all teachers of a particular subject at a particular grade level are obliged to be on the same page of the same text at the same time. It is said, for instance, that this makes it possible for students to change schools without missing a beat.

Although we understand the administrative convenience (and, possibly, the profitability) of mandated, standardized instruction, no intellectually coherent case can be made for a mandate of this sort. It has absolutely no place in the work of any professional, especially those who have to deal with 30 or more dynamic young students, from different backgrounds, who function at different levels, all needing to master complex material that is essential for their success in the world. The analogy might be to require every Little League coach to instruct every player of the same age to pitch in precisely the same way at the same time every Friday afternoon. Individuals who advocate mandated school- or systemwide standardized instruction simply do not understand learning, teaching, administration, leadership, curriculum, assessment, or any other facet of education.

Such factors as the massive explosion in the power of technology, the individual and cultural differences of students, the importance of working with actual student interests and capacities, and the exponential increase in the availability of information, all make standardized instruction absurd. The PrLC format does not apply to programs that fly so much in the face of competent teaching. Our philosophical foundations are simply incompatible with such an approach. We have no doubt that some might wish to use our book and process in an attempt to follow such mandates. We regret that fact, and our process is not suited for that purpose. We believe in the uniqueness of each child and each teacher. Our objective is to create educational communities where people work together while honoring a rich diversity.

Begin by Working on School Climate

Research shows quite conclusively that there is an optimal state of mind for learning. We call it relaxed alertness (see Chapter 1). That is also the optimal state of mind for groups of people to work together to resolve complex issues, which is why we suggest that the first goal for any sustained program of improvement is to develop the right climate in a school.

The PrLC is designed to contribute to the improvement of climate. The use of the process creates a sort of psychological space that makes it easier to solve many other problems.

Consider, for example, the issue of student discipline. First, when communication among staff is effective, it is much easier for people to listen to each other and deal with alternatives in an open-minded way. Second, every issue calls for an examination of fundamental assumptions and a discussion of the evidence in support of the different opinions educators might have about, say, discipline on the playground. The solution may lie with the attitudes and background of students, or with drugs. And it could also lie, in whole or in part, with the approach to instruction that teachers are adopting, with the ways in which they address genuine student interests and concerns, with educator understanding of student differences, and with a host of other issues. The PrLC process makes it easier for these questions to be placed on the table and researched, without just resorting to an exchange of personal beliefs. Third, the process can then be used for brainstorming and problem solving. Research (in the form of solutions found by others) can be introduced, potential solutions can be tried out through the action research process, and the staff can work together to find answers.

Beyond the mere use of the PrLC process itself is the opportunity to use other materials that address climate and relationships. Here is an example from a high school in the Midwest with which we have worked, in which climate and instruction were linked. In the words of the program coordinator, the school

> contextualizes core English language arts and mathematics curricula around the Career Technical Education programs of engineering technology, mechatronics, and multimedia production.

An abiding concern is to maintain a cooperative, respectful climate with high standards. Again in his words,

> A 9th grade text that is a foundation for creating the school culture of student voice and self-reliance is *The 7 Habits of Highly Effective Teens*, by Sean Covey. Using an ordered sharing, the staff shared their views about public education and about their specific content area. We then studied the book so that we all were using common language when speaking about the habits with the students, and we discussed how the concepts in the 7 habits book could be used to establish and reinforce this culture with our students. Then we took the staff's ideas into their classrooms. The students and teachers discussed how paradigms affect behavior and performance in school and in life. This study was followed up with further activities that incorporated the 7 habits as a method for reshaping students' paradigms. In our staff regroupings we reflected in our team meetings about the culture of our center and the impact that our emphasis on this text had on student motivation and achievement.

He added that

> The use of ordered sharing has positively impacted our staff communication, . . . [and] the reflective study has enhanced

the depth of our conversations about learning. But where this process really comes to life, in my mind, is with the instructors' commitment to implement the concepts that were studied into their classroom, and with the real learning that comes from the group's reflection on how the students' achievement was impacted by this change in instruction. (S. Palmer, personal communication, Oct. 16, 2009)

Note that it is in the *doing,* and in the continuous nature of the process, that success is achieved.

Make Any Issue You Select a Big Issue

When we suggest that an issue is a big issue, we are not talking about treating the issue as an urgent crisis. Rather, we encourage participants to use the PrLC to deal with the issue in depth. Our approach is not a matter of simply debating different opinions (although this can happen). Nor is our process largely an opportunity to brainstorm (although at times this *should* happen). Rather, the key is to use the PrLC as an opportunity to genuinely research the issue, examine core assumptions, test skills and approaches, and expand teacher capacity. In the following sections we consider two examples to illustrate the point.

Example 1: Improving Test Scores Generally

One issue on almost every educator's mind is the need to improve test scores. Because accountability is based on test results, this challenge can be approached in at least two different ways. First, we could simply assume that the key to improving test scores is to gather accurate data about student performance on tests and then to teach to the tests with the goal of spending more time on any area of supposed weakness. Note the underlying assumptions here—that test scores accurately assess what students actually know and that directly teaching what is on the tests will result in higher levels of performance over time in sustainable ways. That a large number of schools are currently adopting this approach is understandable, particularly in the face of so much pressure to produce results. But there are many problems with this approach. For instance, Lauren Resnik (2010) writes

> Furthermore, it now seems likely that the accountability regime that appears to be creating much of the improvement in Basic skills may actually be limiting progress towards the kinds of more challenging competencies that we seek. (p. 186)

A second approach would be to research the link between teaching, test scores, and student learning in more depth. This manner of addressing the issue would lead to a deeper grasp of the problem. One huge conceptual blind spot we have as a culture, and that permeates the world of education, is the belief that test scores, genuine understanding, and real-world outcomes are directly linked. They are not. The link is indirect. In essence, when educators teach for real understanding and competence, for the capacity to see connections and deal with change, and more, then students become better prepared (Caine, G., & Caine, R., 2001). And they can then perform better on tests. That is one reason why nations such as Finland do so much better on international comparisons than the United States (OECD, 2006).

The practical implication is that teachers and administrators need to understand the differences between teaching for memorization (surface knowledge) and teaching for understanding (technical/scholastic knowledge). Some attention to the former is quite legitimate. Many strategies are available for helping students memorize basic facts and routines, and it is useful to master some of those strategies, which can act as confidence boosters for some students. However, the larger goal should be to develop the capacity to teach for, and assess, deep understanding. Resnick (2010) therefore calls for a "thinking curriculum."

To teach and assess for deep understanding aligns with what great educators know. When students are taught for understanding and competence, the ultimate test is whether they can solve challenging problems, report on their thinking and their processes, and use their knowledge and skill in the real world. When they can, they will, in fact, also start to perform better on most tests (although some attention to test-taking skills might be warranted). And those increases can be sustained. Examples can be found in many countries, in public education, in charter schools, in home schooling, and at every level from early childhood education to high school.

Example 2: Improving the Teaching of Math

A school we'll call Shadow Ridge is a synthesis of individuals and schools with which we have worked. Consider it to be a large middle school with students from a wide range of social and economic backgrounds. The school is generally well regarded in the community, with some active parent support. But the leadership team and most teachers have been well aware of the need to raise math scores for some time. Informal discussions have taken place for several months, leading to a general consensus about the need to do something.

The principal also has a few stipulations of her own:

• The process is about more than new strategies for memorizing formulas. The students need to understand math—at whatever level they happen to be.

• The program being adopted must be grounded in a solid research base, and part of the program calls for teachers to study and come to understand that research base.

• It is better to do it right than to do it fast and have to do it again. This program will last for at least one year, and perhaps several years, with the goal of building a solid foundation for math instruction in the entire school.

With all this in mind, the principal decides to use a relatively unconventional approach. She decides that the math staff should research and determine for themselves what new approaches to try—and that the PrLC format will be the vehicle for their program.

The First PrLC Meeting

The principal (we will call her Helen) schedules a meeting to formally begin the process. She has a very simple agenda:

- Item 1 is an introduction to the PrLC format.
- Item 2 is the process for selecting the materials to use.

Introducing the PrLC format. After greeting the group, Helen states the purpose of the gathering and the agenda. She hands out a simple description of the PrLC format. It states the core purposes: to foster collaboration, build relationships, promote rigorous learning, and generate results. It includes a one-page overview of the four phases of each meeting, and it spells out the basic time lines. The participants engage in a general discussion about the procedure and indicate a willingness to try it.

Ordered sharing: Prior experience with teaching math. Helen conducts an ordered sharing, beginning with this question: What has been most enjoyable, and what has been least enjoyable, for you in your teaching of math? Staff members think for a moment and then begin to share:

P1: To be honest, I like working with kids who like math, and I get irritated with those who don't get it.

P2: The word problems seem to work sometimes, and I enjoy it when the kids get the bit between their teeth and work on the problem. But I get very frustrated at their struggles to remember basic math symbols and notation.

P3: It's really cool when one of the kids gets it and can explain things to some of the others.

→| |← →| |← →| |← →| |←

Reflective study: Possible materials for professional development. Helen speaks for a few minutes. The gist of her talk is as follows:

> We all know that we need to improve results. And we all know that there are many approaches out there to teaching math. We've agreed that we want to find the best material that we can, and that we want to understand *why* we do the things we do, as well as *what* to do. We've also agreed to take the long view. We know that it would really help to get better results this year, but we can't afford to put too much pressure on ourselves or the students. So we are going to work on a new approach this year, but we will take the time that will be necessary to master it. Right now we need to find a research-based, effective approach that we can all implement. The way we're going to do it is for all of us to start looking for alternatives. We'll report back on what we find and basically agree together on what to use. Then we'll use this group process to work through it.

The participants begin to brainstorm. They identify a number of possible ways to proceed: doing online searches for programs and materials, searching for books and articles, talking to other teachers or schools that have faced a similar challenge to see what they did, examining any programs that they can get their hands on, and talking to really good math teachers that they know.

Commitment to action: Research. The participants collectively parcel out tasks and agree to get back together in two weeks at the same place and time.

Regrouping. Helen decides that this is a good time to introduce the regrouping phase of the process. She suggests that it is now time to review what has been decided. In the process of doing this, all the action items are summarized. She also suggests that it might be useful to reflect on how they had worked together. She leads staff through an ordered sharing in which each person in turn reviews what stood out from the meeting and how they had worked together.

The Second PrLC Meeting

Two weeks later the staff members meet again, and they spend a brief period of time on general discussion and some venting about frustrations.

Helen calls the group together and conducts an *ordered sharing*. She introduces the subject that will be discussed by making the following request: Briefly summarize what you did, and share something about what most interested or surprised you.

P1: I went online and found a *huge* amount of material. But it was difficult to find anything with the sort of depth we are looking for. I found one interesting approach that they use in the Netherlands called "Reality Math Education" that I want to talk about.

P2: I took the easy route. I called a friend of mine who teaches math educators. She gave me a couple of books that look good. I've brought one today for us to look at.

P3: I looked at what some schools are doing and found myself thinking about assessment. It's pretty clear that we have to have some way to have students reveal their actual thinking and show what they can do. This will never fly if all we do is look at test results.

The discussion continues with other participants making their contributions.

The *reflective study* becomes the way to examine what they found and dig deeper. The group members talk through the materials that have been brought to the discussion. They collectively go online as necessary. They also thumb through some books. One is Sousa's *How the Brain Learns Mathematics* (2008). Another is *Teaching for Deep Understanding* (Leithwood, McAdie, Bascia, & Rodrigue, 2006), which has a specific chapter on teaching math.

The *commitment to action* takes the form of deciding that *Teaching for Deep Understanding* will become their foundational text for at least the next year and that they will browse through it before the next meeting. They agree to supplement that primary text with other material from time to time.

The participants agree on logistics for the next few meetings. The meeting finishes with a *regrouping* in which, one by one, all the participants reflect briefly on the process and what they look forward to doing in the months to come.

From this point on, the PrLC format is followed as precisely as possible.

Noteworthy Points from Shadow Ridge

The Shadow Ridge example illustrates several points worth noting, including the following:

• The principal introduced the process in a gentle way. She provided an overview of the structure at the first meeting, together with an ordered sharing and a regrouping. Once the participants had reviewed the basic materials and agreed to the logistics, the full process was introduced.

• Helen knew that it was important to stay focused and to "hold" the entire process in her mind to ensure that each step was taken, even though the format was not as precise as it would be in the meetings to follow.

• The approach in *Teaching for Deep Understanding* has been researched in its own right and has produced positive results. Its view of learning and teaching aligns with the approach described in this book. That alignment suggests that, when coupled with the PrLC format, the results at Shadow Ridge will be very good.

• Note that several interconnected issues emerged. The group paid attention, either directly or indirectly, to subject-matter content, how students learn, how to teach, assessment and test scores, staff buy-in and collaboration, and staff communication.

• If they desired, the group could have had another meeting or two before making a final decision.

The critical point is that it is essential to go through each facet of the PrLC format, and to honor the purpose and protocols of each facet, to deal with the issue adequately.

11

Results

A Crystal-Clear Purpose for Education: Develop great human beings to be contributors (not burdens) to society.

—*The Human Greatness Group*

In exploring process learning circles, we need to consider two types of results. The first is the extent to which the PrLCs do create authentic professional learning communities, which can be revealed through quotes and indicators of changes in behavior among those in a school or a group using the process. The second is to consider how that community is reflected in the academic results of students. And because test scores are on everyone's mind, the logical question is, Does the process help to raise test scores? The short answer is yes—provided the process is appropriately implemented and the nature of test scores is understood. The issue is complicated because many factors are at work.

What Test Results Reveal

In the present climate, results on standardized tests often simply reflect teaching for memorization and not any other outcome (such as genuine understanding of concepts). It is relatively easy to raise test scores in some subject areas in the short term by implementing new techniques for memorization and shallow understanding. Unfortunately, these results are virtually impossible to sustain, and they build little foundation for attaining higher standards in the medium and long term.

Paradoxically, there is a better way to use tests, and that is as a *secondary* mode of assessment. When teachers teach for understanding or meaning, success is best revealed by whether or not students can solve problems or use material in new and different ways. Some tests can be designed to assess some of this, but most tests are not that sophisticated. However, when students do demonstrate more advanced academic competence through authentic assessment, they also tend to perform better on standardized tests.

Individual research supports this notion (see, e.g., Leithwood et al., 2006), as do systemwide programs in place in various locations (see, e.g., the results of Finnish students on PISA and other international tests, available at http://www.pisa2006.helsinki.fi/index.htm; and the results of Learning to Learn in South Australia, Department of Education and Children's Services [DECS], 2004). We have demonstrated the same sorts of results in our work, as we describe in this chapter.

We are passionately committed to teaching for understanding as a basic minimum throughout the K–12 system. Test scores then rise, and at the same time a foundation is built that increases the likelihood of long-term success and productive human development.

We understand the pressure behind adopting simplistic programs in the heat of the moment—and doing so may produce some short-term rises in test scores. But this usually occurs at enormous cost, including the reduction in time spent on subjects that are not covered on high-stakes assessments.

So although the goal of raising test scores is quite legitimate in the present climate, we all need to be wary about what test results actually mean. It is always important and useful, therefore, to look for other indicators of success.

The essential point for our purposes is that programs and processes need to work together and be supported by the system. As we show in Chapter 1, for instance, threat rigidity or downshifting interferes with success. Thus an otherwise excellent program or process can fail if, for instance, the administration ignores or belittles it, which is why we strongly suggest that administrators actively participate in the PrLC process. In our view, nothing demonstrates commitment to a process more than active participation in it. With these caveats in mind, the following sections describe four situations in which the PrLC format was used with great success.

Examples from the Field

The following examples are drawn from our personal experiences with schools and programs beginning in 1992.

Dry Creek Elementary

As described in Chapter 1, in 1992 we were invited to work with Dry Creek Elementary, a small, low-socioeconomic, K–6 school just outside Sacramento, California. Dry Creek was where we first formulated and implemented what have become PrLCs in a multiyear program. Here are some comments from staff members (Caine, R., & Caine, G., 1997a):

- "I'm remembering myself as a child."
- "It's great getting to know group members in a new way."
- "I have never felt like a part of the whole (THE GLOBAL WHOLE) as I have since we started the process. If I can give one student this experience I will feel like I have accomplished something."

Parents and visitors also made highly positive comments, and their observations were confirmed by changes in behavior. One example is parent participation in PTA meetings, with attendance increasing from zero to more than 40 parents. The school also experienced a significant drop in vandalism and discipline problems.

We should note that the school's beloved principal left after the process had been in effect for three years, and a series of other problems emerged related to resources, district issues, and the dilution of the practices that had been developed. Discipline problems also began to increase. This led to the decision to renew the process, an action that promoted a general sense of relief. In one unsolicited letter, a teacher wrote the following:

> We may have lost our "field" when we lost our process groups. It "feels" different already as we come together under the old process group framework.... Participation is crucial for adults and students. I'm working on being more of a participant. (Caine, R., & Caine, G., 1997a, p. 233)

As for test scores in that three-year period when the PrLCs were fully implemented, between February 1993 and May 1995, scores moved from the 50th to the 60th percentile in 1st grade reading, and from the 49th to the 55th percentile in 2nd grade reading; by February 1996, they had increased to the 79th percentile for 1st grade and the 74th percentile for 2nd grade. Math scores also increased, although not as dramatically. And these results were sustained.

Park View Middle School

Park View was a new school in Southern California, and the process of getting up and running included a great deal of turbulence. The "D-track" (one of four tracks) elected to use our process and work with us. The experience was not always smooth (see Chapter 13), but the results mirrored what had happened at Dry Creek. One teacher wrote the following:

> There is a recognizable difference that is lasting and genuine within D-track. We had become angry. But now we've shifted to empowering ourselves and not blaming others for the elements we want to change. We became more responsible. It was a genuine shift in how we saw ourselves and the school. Our desire was not to manipulate the school, but to take ownership for and of ourselves. (Caine, R., & Caine, G., 1997a, p. 211)

And another teacher had this to say:

> Part of growing came with sharing with others—the people. Now I see where I have short-changed the kids. This opens more doors for me. I don't feel alone. For years I have felt alone. (Caine, R., & Caine, G., 1997a, p. 211)

Academic results at the school also improved significantly. Grade-point averages increased by one point for all students in D-track, and failure rates dropped from 20 percent to below 8 percent (despite the fact that 28 percent of the students were special needs students who were mainstreamed). Results on the California Test of Basic Skills (the statewide standardized test) could not be attributed (either positively or negatively) to the process for several reasons, one of which is that the timing of 8th grade tests meant that the students had also been taught by teachers who were not part of the process. However, California also had a voluntary standardized algebra test, and over a two-year period, the number of students from Park View choosing to take the test doubled, with most volunteers coming from D-track. And of those students from the school receiving the Golden State Award for scoring high in algebra, 45 percent came from D-track, with each of the other tracks averaging just 18 percent.

Rose Warren Empowerment School

Rose Warren is a K–6 empowerment school in Las Vegas that had been designated as being in need of improvement. The student population numbers about 670. Of these, 76.1 percent are Hispanic/Latino, 13.5 percent are white/Caucasian, 6.7 percent are African American, and 3.4 percent are Asian/Pacific Islander. Three-quarters of the students qualify for free lunches, and 57 percent are ESL students. The PrLC format was introduced at the beginning of the 2008–09 school year following a phone call to Renate from the principal, who had attended a five-day workshop with her more than 10 years earlier.

In 2009, the school improved in every category (with the single exception of 3rd grade math) after our first year together. The school met its target and found safe harbor. Indeed, it was the most successful empowerment school in the county. The 4th grade English language arts trend data showed an increase in the percentage of age-grade proficiency from 35 percent to 45 percent. The improvement in math was prodigious, with a jump from 48 percent to 76 percent being proficient. Fifth grade improvements were also clear in English language arts (increasing from 26 to 32 percent proficiency) and math (49 to 52 percent). And the jump in 5th grade students being proficient in science was 19 points—from 27 to 46 percent. Even more exciting was the increase in writing proficiency. The school outperformed all schools in the district and the state. Overall the school achieved 68.6 percent proficiency in ideas, 66.1 percent proficiency in writing, and 66.1 percent proficiency in voice.

Now let's look at some of the other factors that were involved. The principal was a superb leader. Under her guidance, the school had embarked on a change program two years before our process was introduced. It had been working with at least two other programs that focused on reading and math. It had access to excellent technology (the whole school was wired, and even students in 1st and 2nd grade were working with laptop computers). And for the most part, the principal had selected excellent teachers. So what did we add?

In the opinion of the principal, of lead teachers, and of the independent assessment team, the PrLC format contributed significantly to the sense of community in the school and the ways in which staff worked together. It dovetailed well with the other programs and the general approach of the principal. And it added to a sense of rigor in the ways that staff thought about what they were doing and thus helped to improve the other programs the school had adopted. So it contributed to a general improvement in teaching and in the climate of the school, but it was not the only factor in the overall scheme of things. Unfortunately, owing to lack of funds available, all programs were substantially reduced in 2009.

Redwood School

Redwood Elementary School in Fontana, California, was a low-socioeconomic, low-performing K–5 elementary school with more than 1,000 students, 89 percent of whom were Hispanic. The school operated on a multitrack, year-round calendar. The school site was in an industrial environment with a fertilizer factory next door.

Two administrators came to us because they were concerned that in an effort to implement district standards, teachers at their school were sacrificing the more complex, constructivist teaching advocated by the *California Standards for the Teaching Profession* (July, 1997). Teachers were opting for simplified direct instruction, focusing extensively on memory of isolated, decontextualized facts and skills through rote practice and rehearsal, or "teaching to the test." The administrators felt that our work could help teachers maintain a constructivist focus even as they attempted to raise reading comprehension test scores. And so for one year (2001), Renate implemented the PrLC format systematically. (For a full report, see Caine, R., 2008.)

Leadership. One of the two administrators on site was fully committed and provided superb leadership throughout. She supported the teachers, participated in the process, monitored proceedings, made the decision that this would be the major professional development program the staff would be engaged in for the year, and generally invested a great deal of energy in the entire process.

Participation. Although the school offered incentives for teachers to attend the workshops and participate in the program, ultimately participation was voluntary. The assistant principal, who was totally committed to the process, also participated in it.

Selection of materials. The content was the brain/mind learning principles we had developed (see Appendix A). Renate introduced one principle a month, as the focal point for professional development. Participants were exposed to the theory, developed practical implications and strategies to try out in their classrooms, and came back to their process learning circles with feedback (documentation) and to share their reflections.

It was not possible to cover the entire set of 12 principles in one year (although that remains our ideal). The Redwood School PrLC dealt with the first 7 principles.

Procedures. The program was kicked off with an intensive, day-long introductory meeting at which the process was introduced and modeled, and a series of monthly meetings were planned. Tuesdays had been designated minimum school days, and students were dismissed at noon, giving teachers the rest of the day to meet in teams and plan together. Renate met on the first Tuesday of each month with all teachers and staff members who had volunteered to participate. That meeting followed the PrLC format.

Because the school operations were year-round, almost all teachers missed the introduction to at least one principle. Several teachers, however, chose to attend these workshops while they were officially off campus.

During the second and fourth Tuesdays of each month, teachers met in other PrLCs to conduct other school business. In these groups, teachers also had the opportunity to further discuss the principle under investigation for that month and to share what they were doing in their classes.

On one other Tuesday each month, Renate also visited the school. She was available for classroom observations in the morning. Discussions and feedback were handled on a sign-up basis in the afternoon.

Results. We were delighted with evidence of positive change on two fronts: (1) a shift in the learning community of educators and (2) the improvement of student scores on standardized tests.

Comments made by teachers two months into the process referred to the shift in conversations that teachers had with each other. Comments like the following were frequent: "I truly feel like a professional because we find ourselves talking about learning and what we are doing with students." Such statements were accompanied by others that reflected a change in the nature of how teachers listened to and worked with each other. Here are two typical examples: "With my colleagues, we have begun listening to each other more quietly and carefully in meetings (I'm still working on it)." Also, "My colleagues have begun to team teach" (Caine, R., 2008, p. 139).

In terms of test scores, the original goals for the school included a growth target gain of 16 points on the SAT9 for the 2001–02 school year as measured by the Academic Performance Index (California state standards). The school's actual growth amounted to 48 points, far exceeding the target. In addition, Hispanic students, whose target growth base had been set at 13 points, ended up with actual growth of 54 points. Moreover, students identified as coming from low-socioeconomic environments and disadvantaged also exceeded their target. Their target had been set at 13 points, and their actual growth was 47 points.

Sustainability. The program described here was discontinued when both administrators left the school. The school subsequently had four different principals over a five-year period, but a personal phone call to the principal (J. Dekall, personal communication, Sept. 2006) indicated that the PrLC process had built a very strong sense of community among the staff that helped to hold the teaching approach in place.

Other Stories About Creating Community

The PrLC format has been used in many different ways to build professional learning communities. Here are some other examples:

• An independent school district in Texas used the process for a year with all the administrators in the district. The director of curriculum, who led the project, had the process researched independently through the University of Houston. The (unpublished) report showed a significant improvement in the ways in which school administrators worked together (J. Stevens, personal communication, 1996).

• A district superintendent in California, who was also an adjunct professor at a local college, used the process in a course that he taught. Both he and the participants felt that it contributed enormously to the depth of their study (D. Johnson, personal communication, May 14, 2010).

- A staff member of a philanthropic foundation has recently begun to use the process with school administrators and more than 200 teachers who are learning in Communities of Practice. They are extremely enthusiastic and are looking at ways to implement the process in their schools (J. Lawrence, personal communication, May 28, 2010).

- Senior staff in the Macomb Intermediate School District in Michigan used aspects of the process as a common understanding and way to work together for several years.

Clearly the process morphs and can be adapted to a wide variety of situations. The key is to follow it systematically and rigorously at the beginning, and to master the philosophy behind it. When the process morphs after years of use, it retains its underlying integrity—and power.

part III

Advanced Keys
to Success

12

Individual Differences

The concept of diversity encompasses acceptance and respect.... It is about understanding each other and moving beyond simple tolerance to embracing and celebrating the rich dimensions of diversity contained within each individual.

—University of Oregon Diversity Initiative

Although the process in the book can be used with every adult in a school or district, people are also individuals. We are alike, and we are different. This means that leaders and participants will interpret the process differently, they will value various aspects of it differently, and they will respond to each other and to the group differently.

These differences are both a blessing and a burden. They enrich the process and the learning enormously. And they are the source of disagreements and conflicts. So one of the challenges for every process leader, and everyone who works with groups and in a community, is to get a handle on how people are different.

Background

Individual differences are the topic of a wealth of research and a world of psychology. They can be framed in terms of differences in personality, learning styles, identity, motivation, and many other characteristics.

Perhaps the best-known instrument is the Myers-Briggs Type Indicator (Briggs Myers & McCaulley, 1985), which is available for adults. It assesses preferences in how people perceive the world and make decisions and is based on a psychological theory developed by Carl Jung.

Other learning-styles instruments are based on which senses predominate in an individual, an approach that was first popularized through a methodology called neurolinguistic programming (Bandler & Grinder, 1975). They seek to determine whether people learn predominately in auditory, visual, or kinesthetic ways.

Another approach has been the attempt to reconceive intelligence. Among the pioneers doing this work are Howard Gardner (1993, 2006) with his work on multiple intelligences, and Robert Sternberg (1985) with his work on three primary types of intelligence.

The vast array of approaches can be confusing. The difficulty is compounded by the fact that groups and societies can also be so different. And yet it is really useful to have some tools that help us read others and ourselves, so that we can make sense of general patterns of behavior.

The Caine Identity Profile

In the early 1990s the two of us synthesized patterns from a wide range of instruments and some personal work that we had done in previous years to create a tool that we call an identity profile. It describes some general patterns of perception and behavior. We researched it for construct validity and have used it many times with educators and with students. It helps to explain some of the different ways in which people function in groups and relate to each other. That makes it useful in team building—and in developing a learning community.

Our profile outlines four different types of identity. We call them *Evaluators*, *Nurturers*, *Directors*, and *Adventurers*. Every individual has aspects of all of the four types, but most of our perceptions and actions are driven by the characteristic that predominates. (See Figure 12.1.)

Figure 12.1

Four Identity Types in the Caine Identity Profile

Evaluator
- Vision dominates.
- Loves order and system.
- Can be "picky."
- Is rigid when under pressure.

Nurturer
- Emotions and touch dominate.
- Loves relationship and detail, and tends to follow.
- Can be "clingy."
- Is overly sensitive under pressure.

Director
- Sound dominates.
- Loves big picture and taking charge.
- Can be "bossy."
- Applies pressure when under pressure.

Adventurer
- No one sense dominates, though smell and taste are really important.
- Loves variety.
- Can be "flighty."
- Becomes scattered under pressure.

Note: The Caine Identity Profile can be found in more detail online at http://www.cainelearning.com/files/Bookstore.html. For a small fee, you can download the profile and have it scored; results returned within 24 hours (weekdays).

Naturally the types overlap; it is important to be careful not to view them as too rigid or absolute. However, they do help adults (and students) see some of the patterns they have in common with others and to highlight differences.

Evaluators

Vision dominates in members of this group, and seeing is very important for understanding. How things look—either in the real world or in their minds—is also important. This means that pictures and visuals are important means of communicating with them. Evaluators can also be identified because their language is full of words that convey sight, such as "I see" or "that's clear" or "it's a bit murky." Body language, facial expressions, and avoiding obstructions to vision are all important to them.

The Evaluators' emphasis on vision is accompanied by a delight in order and system. They plan ahead of time and like to follow their plans. They are most likely to read instructions (before just trying things out) and will want to follow those instructions precisely. So Evaluators are the people most likely to want to be very systematic about the guidelines for the process learning circles and most likely to be bothered when someone deviates from the prescribed approach.

Their need for clarity and precision can show up in perfectionism and a need to deal with details, to the point where others think they are "picky." This attention to order and detail can be a superb asset—it helps to ensure that everything that needs to be done is done, and that it is done right. And it can be a liability, because it can slow things down too much and because focusing too much on the details can obscure the big picture and reduce flexibility.

For the purposes of facilitation, the Evaluators are really important in preserving the integrity and system of a process, but they often need to loosen up a bit and discern when to go with the flow.

Nurturers

Emotions and touch dominate in Nurturers, and touching and feeling are important for understanding. Relationships and feelings—both their own and how they imagine others feel—are extremely important to them. That means that tactile and physical experiences, as well as connecting with others, help them grasp ideas. They need people around them and can become depressed and morose when alone or when they feel that they are alone.

Nurturers are natural followers. Because they care so much, they like to help others. They work hard for causes that they believe in. They are more likely to follow and support, rather than to lead, because they see this as a way of helping and supporting others. Thus they are likely to become very committed to a group or a program. They can also be anxious to please, with the implication that they can also be quick to feel rejected and have their feelings hurt, which then leads to withdrawal.

Nurturers like details and can become frustrated if there are not enough instructions. They also like close connection with a leader. Similarly, process leaders who are Nurturers like close connections with the members of a group. The challenge here is that when relationships get too close, it can be difficult to be professional and stay detached enough to ensure that a process or project is working appropriately.

In a group, Nurturers can be invaluable as some of those who actively build relationships, invite others in, and generally help people to feel at ease. This becomes a burden at times, because they do not want others to feel hurt, and so Nurturers might intervene to stop what they sense is "hard" questioning. Doing so may lead to the avoidance of the required struggle for real understanding and the important learning that people develop through facing themselves. So a primary challenge for Nurturers is to develop strong personal boundaries and to allow others to have their own learning experiences.

Directors

Sound dominates for Directors, and words and sounds are very important to understanding. Members of this group need to understand before acting. They tend to use words like "tune in" or "I hear you" or "that sounds like such-and-such"; so using the right words and enough words is important in communicating with them. However, Directors do not like too much detail, preferring the big picture in a structured form; and so spending too much time on detail (for them) can trigger impatience.

Directors are natural leaders. They like the facts, they like big challenges, and they like to take charge. These qualities can be invaluable. The downside is that they can focus on the task at the expense of relationship, and they can put excessive pressure on people to get things done (though they do not like being put under pressure themselves). They like to accomplish things, and they enjoy completing difficult tasks.

In communication they tend to be direct and blunt. In groups, Directors can be wonderful assets because they can—and do—"tell it like it is." However, in doing that, they can miss or puncture a slowly unfolding relationship or process. So their challenge is to relax into the chaos a little, and to acquire a little more compassion for the struggles that people have and the indirect and messy feelings and the lack of direction that tend to occur when groups of people are doing complex things.

Adventurers

Adventurers love change and variety, and they tend to enjoy the sensations of life. No one sense dominates, although smell and taste are important. Because they like to experiment, they tend to act before reading instructions and to try things out to see what works. They are also quite happy to shift, and may even change what seems to be working, just for the fun of doing something different.

They are not overly concerned about the authority of others, although they frequently find themselves in the front and leading what is happening. This occurs as much out of interest in what is going to happen as in knowing what actually has to happen.

Adventurers tend to enjoy people. They like stories, tell jokes, and are willing to clown around. This capacity can work wonders for loosening a group and helping people to enjoy the moment. But the downside is that they may not take procedures and protocols seriously, which can be an obstacle to the development of expertise and to success.

Adventurers have a mixed relationship with projects. They are quite willing and eager to try something new—an invaluable asset for a group. However, they can get bored and then will not see something through to completion. They are capable of immense flexibility and can often adapt quickly to change. Their challenge is to develop discernment, so that they know when to play and when to respect and support procedures that are important to others.

The Effect of Stress

Together, the four styles are a useful tool in dealing with stressed people and stressful situations. As noted in Chapter 1, when people are under a great deal of stress and threat, and a sense of helplessness prevails, the survival response kicks in and people downshift. The result is that they revert to more instinctual behaviors and attitudes and behaviors that were programmed early in life. However, the four styles respond to threat in different but predictable and observable ways. Understanding those differences provides those in a community with an additional set of tools for working with people who feel threatened.

Evaluators

Evaluators tend not to be very flexible at the best of times. When under stress, they can become rigid in their adherence to "the rules." This kind of response makes it very difficult to find compromises, and that is when the best (getting it "just right") becomes the enemy of the good (doing what works). Going along with being a perfectionist can be a type of negativity that puts a damper on attempts to change things. A perfectionist under stress is not a happy camper.

The effect on PrLCs (and other communities and relationships) is to make them overly severe, serious, and rule bound. And, of course, a similar rigidity can show up in the classroom and in leadership. Thus a style that is extraordinarily valuable in setting and aspiring to high standards can become its own worst enemy, by demanding "correct" behaviors when they are not warranted.

Nurturers

Because Nurturers love relationship and supporting others, their response to stress is to feel hurt and to seek to "make things better." The unfortunate consequence is that they can push too close to others and not allow enough space for situations to be dealt with, and they can subvert the truth in their attempts to heal wounded feelings. So being "caring" becomes a veil for "making bad feelings go away."

The effect on PrLCs (and other communities and relationships) is to neutralize and undermine hard-headed analysis of a situation. Being nice substitutes for being realistic, and that can interfere enormously with genuine learning, in part because others are deprived of authentic feedback from the Nurturers. This hurts them as teachers and leaders, because hard issues and real needs are sometimes painful, and the pain needs to be directly addressed.

Directors

Because Directors naturally look at the big picture, tend to place facts over relationships, and take the lead to make things happen, when they become stressed they become bossy and distant. Feelings and relationships may become almost totally irrelevant, and they may brush aside the opinions of others as sometimes seeming less than stupid. Directors under pressure put others under pressure, and their expectations can be so high as to be absurd.

The effect on PrLCs (and other communities and relationships) is to almost brutalize the situation and eliminate nuance and subtlety. Talking *at* people is substituted for talking *with* people, and the Director's opinion is treated as the best, and sometimes only, way to proceed. This behavior can sabotage Directors' teaching and leading because students and colleagues resist such behavior.

Adventurers

Because Adventurers love variety and change, when they get into the survival mode they can become difficult to pin down and cannot be relied upon to complete projects or do what they promise to do. At the same time, they can be very quick to reframe situations and suggest other options without having or taking the time to check them out first. And they tend not to respect or take seriously others' attempts to keep things on track.

The effect on PrLCs (and other communities and relationships) is to fragment and undermine them. Adventurers may disregard protocols, punctuate respectful listening with jokes, and make private affairs public and the butt of jokes. At that point, what may seem like "fun" can impede genuine learning. Moreover, in the role of leaders, downshifted Adventurers may lose a great deal of respect and prestige.

Versatility and Adaptability

The challenge to leaders and educators in dealing with these various identities is twofold. First, we need to know ourselves. We have to grasp some of our core patterns in order to appreciate our strengths and weaknesses, and to progress beyond them. The process of regrouping can be extraordinarily helpful here. Our styles play themselves out in every situation in which we find ourselves—in personal relationships, teaching, meetings, social gatherings, managing projects, and more. As a result, we have many opportunities to notice ourselves in action ("Wow, I'm being too picky here" or "He really bucked when I got too bossy," or "I'm pleased I organized things so well"), and after action as we reflect on how a meeting or project went ("I just don't need to get into all that detail" or "I'm going to see this through to completion if it kills me," or "I connected well with people today and still got everything done").

Second, we need to become more agile and versatile. Our own mode of behavior seems normal, often to the point where other ways of being are treated as aberrations. We may intellectually understand different patterns but still have great difficulty in responding well to them. Great leaders, teachers, parents, and partners need to work at walking in the shoes of others and adapting (at least to some extent) to other ways of being. Evaluators, for instance, need to grasp and accept the fact that a violation of protocols is not necessarily a disaster. And Adventurers need to grit their teeth and appreciate the importance, on many occasions, of system and order. To get to that point, regrouping is the first step; and then attempting to act differently is the second.

→| |← →| |← →| |← →| |←

In Chapter 1 we suggested that in professional development two different but parallel processes are taking place all the time: professional learning and personal learning. In this regard, there is no end to the depth in which one can investigate the profiles. Indeed, this subject could be a marvelous yearlong project for a PrLC, and it would benefit participants in every aspect of their lives, including education.

13

Group Dynamics

Group development is characterized by periods of relative calm punctuated by intervals of chaotic activity. This periodicity is essential for growth and reorganization because, without undergoing periodic upheaval, groups cannot evolve.

—Bud A. McClure, author

Although educators often do not like the word, group work is *messy*. Participants do not always want to do the same thing. They often miscommunicate. They interpret language (including guidelines) in different ways. Logistical problems arise from time to time. And weaving throughout it all is a complex set of relationships and individual reactions to everything from what a person says to whether a person is liked or disliked.

In short, stuff happens.

In addition, as people work together over time, a group identity forms. The group takes on a mind and a character of its own.

All of this can be expected. And being aware of it can help a process leader and a group to keep on a relatively even keel and navigate through the process.

As we have noted earlier, one reason for following the protocols that have been spelled out in this book is that together they help to build a container—a space within which the process happens. Containers have boundaries (though they can be quite porous). And containers have a location in space and time. The very fact of putting these containers in place helps to provide support and stability for the process that is to take place.

Note that one role of the process leader, then, is to protect the container. A way to describe this is "holding the space" or "holding the energy." This is done by remaining focused and being present, no matter what is going on (though we all fall off the horse occasionally!).

It's important to realize that some initial turbulence is natural. When people get together for the first time, no matter how well intentioned, they need to do some "negotiating" and deal with many different sets of expectations. This reality means that it just takes time to settle down and begin to work together. It also means that there will be times of quiet and times of activity, times of boredom and times of excitement, times of feeling connected and times of feeling alienated. That's just the way it is.

Here's how Cindy Tucker, the principal of Dry Creek, described the early stage of the PrLC process:

> At this point, we're in the process of becoming a learning community. Our study groups are meeting regularly, and after some adjustments and refinements, everyone has a home. There are layers upon layers of feelings, some interesting conversations, questions and comments, insights and connections. I think we're right on track with the change process as we experience a mixture of exhilaration, exhaustion, determination, uncertainty, reluctance, and passion. (Caine, R., & Caine, G., 1997a, p. 197)

Phases in the Formation of a Group

Although the formation of groups entails an ebb and a flow, over time groups begin to gel. Many people have discerned patterns in this process. None of the patterns is absolute, nor is there any magic to them. However, it is useful to keep these possibilities in mind because they can help to move things along.

One of the most popular patterns of group formation over days, weeks, and months is summed up in the phrase *forming, storming, norming, and reforming* (originally coined by Tuckman in 1965, though for him the fourth stage was *performing*). Our experience with education has led us to change Tuckman's sequence and definitions slightly, so we place *norming* before *storming*. Here is our interpretation of the pattern:

• *Forming*—This stage involves all the work that is done from initiating the group process to meeting together the first time (and maybe more than once). It is what has to happen for the personnel to become settled, and for determining the time and place, framing the purpose, and addressing other logistical issues (including decisions about facilitation and leadership).

• *Norming*—This stage overlaps with the later stages of forming, with the key being that essential protocols and processes are set in place. In our case, the four phases of the process learning circle format are clarified and accepted, so the participants are building the container and creating its borders. They have accepted the basic process principles (e.g., begin and end on time). They agree with various principles such as the notion that the circle is to be a safe place and that what happens in the circle is not to be discussed outside. Not all norms can be spelled out, but the gist of what will happen becomes clear.

• *Storming*—In this stage, tensions develop, disagreements surface, commitment varies. People may come and go. In other words, as the work begins, reality sets in and people experience and express their differing reactions. These need to be dealt with. Sometimes it will be in a discussion of the whole group. Sometimes the process leader will need to meet with an individual participant. Sometimes a few participants need to get together to talk things through. Sometimes it is just a matter of riding things out. And sometimes there is no "storming" at all, but it is simply apparent that people are participating on the surface and not really digging into the learning. These issues need to be dealt with and are usually a major growing point for both the process leader and the participants. As one teacher recollected in our work with Park View Middle School:

> In the process groups, we had struggles and breakdowns but we made that commitment to keep this going. It is a part of any relationship. (Caine, R., & Caine, G., 1997a, p. 209)

• *Reforming*—After some time, things settle down. The protocols are taken for granted. Participants begin to support the process. The introduction of new material and the treatment of old material occur as a kind of flow. And so, in general, a set of values and norms fall into place so that much of what the group does is self-governing and self-sustaining. Once this has happened, occasional moments of tension are often resolved by the group itself without needing intervention by the process leader. And the group begins to take on an identity and a life and mind of its own. (As mentioned earlier, sometimes the fourth stage is called *performing*.)

In practice, the four phases never occur this cleanly and clearly, and they may sometimes be repeated. The important point is not to get flustered when things are not going perfectly. The task of the process leader and participants is to work through the process.

Process Checks and Assumption Checks

Two tools are of great value when a hiccup occurs in the process, leading to some tension or conflict. They can be used by anyone, not just the process leader. One is a *process check* and the other is an *assumption check*.

Process Checks

When things seem to be substantially out of kilter, it may be time for someone to call for a process check. Just as the name implies, this is a moment when other activity stops, and the group collectively focuses attention on the group dynamic itself. "What is happening here?" The key is for participants to sense how they are feeling and to begin to describe what is happening—but not in a judgmental way.

It is when people notice what's up that the energy in the group can change and the process can move on. It may be, for instance, that someone is upset and needs to take a break. It may be that an announcement was made that had a huge effect on participants and that needs to be addressed.

We remember once when we were conducting a workshop for the entire staff in a school near Monterey, California, and wondering where their attention was. It turns out that some of them were going to be receiving pink slips the afternoon of our workshop! Such a situation is not conducive to effective professional development. On another occasion we were conducting a workshop for principals in North Carolina. Halfway through the event the state superintendent walked in and asked us to leave. He then told each of the principals what their school scores had been, read them the riot act (we were told), and then walked out. This situation also was not conducive to a good workshop atmosphere.

Don't spend too much time on or get too obsessive about dealing with "what's happening." But do be honest and real. The key is to deal with the protocols and to be clear about what it is the group is trying to do.

Assumption Checks

Assumption checks are used when people seem to be arguing across each other, or making rebuttals to claims that were not really made. In essence, people are talking about different things or making different assumptions about a variety of issues, without being aware of the fact.

An assumption check can be called for if the entire group seems to be caught up in the dynamics of miscommunication. Or it can be a tool to use in a discussion between two or three people. One way to proceed is for one party to ask for an assumption check, and then to state what he thinks is being assumed. Here's an example:

It seems to me that you assume I am opposing [something]. Is that what you believe? Because I am not arguing that at all. Let's just double-check what we are dealing with.

The Field of Listening

The entire PrLC process is geared toward creating the field of listening described in Chapter 2 (and explained in more depth in Appendix B). At times communication will be on the surface, but at other times the group descends into the place where the flow of meaning occurs—the space where participants no longer feel a need to compete for time because they know that there will be enough. They recognize that there is no need to defend their point of view, even if they have a personal need to express it. People can have opinions and also feel free to change their minds at any time. Participants are open to the possibility that fundamentally new insights and ideas may emerge. And they share a sense of relationship—a sense of connectedness—in which genuine respect flourishes.

This kind of evolution happens—not always and not all the time, but more and more as the process is implemented. And it is an exciting and rejuvenating place to be.

Small Groups, Large Community

Note that we have been talking only about individual PrLCs. In very small schools or other organizations, the entire staff can be included in one process learning circle. That option generally will not work in larger schools or organizations, primarily because of time constraints and the number of participants.

However, when a single group forms from within a large faculty, or when several groups form, it is possible for cliques to develop because people naturally tend to bond with each other in the groups. The groups themselves may feel separate (and sometimes superior). And at the same time they can be the focus of disdain by others who are not participating in such groups.

In one of the first schools we worked with, Park View Middle School, one track (the term used by the school to distinguish four entities within it) relished the thought of trying our process, but the other three were disinterested. We were quite happy to proceed with D-track, and a small grant made the work possible. As time went by, we were delighted with the track's progress (which we describe in Chapter 11) and did not bother to inquire about the rest of the school. So we were totally surprised when the process leader in D-track told us that the participants had begun to meet secretly and to keep the locations of the meeting private, because the rest of the school regarded them as "elitist" and "above everyone else." Until that point we had simply disregarded the effect that a program within a program could have on the larger school community.

Our goal is not to simply create small groups of educators who work together well. The larger goal is to improve community in the school *as a whole*. Accomplishing this goal requires finding a balance between the individual PrLCs and the larger community. Here are five suggestions to make that happen:

1. If more than one learning circle has been formed, invite the members of all the groups to gather collectively in staff meetings on a regular basis. At those meetings, ask people to talk with participants from other groups, and give them some time to share about their experiences in those groups (however, personal disclosures should be avoided in these collective gatherings). In general, this approach breaks down barriers and helps everyone feel that they are all working on the effort together, even if they bond more closely with the small group of people they meet with regularly.

2. If the majority of staff members have not yet committed to participating in the entire process learning circle format, it is still appropriate and useful to use some of the specific processes with the entire group. For instance, we often find principals who use the first aspect of the group process—the way of listening and talking that we call ordered sharing (see Chapter 5)—as a way to begin staff

meetings. In this way, some core practices and attitudes can be introduced to the staff as a whole.

3. Staff members come and go. Every year new members are added who are unfamiliar with the culture and conditions and practices in a school. In Dry Creek Elementary, for instance, in just the second year of our time together, two of the teachers who had been participating in the process voluntarily undertook to conduct a process learning circle for new teachers who were joining the school staff. We strongly recommend this action step. We suggest that newcomers be invited to participate in a newly formed PrLC to be facilitated (at least in the early stages) by one or two people who have some experience with them. In this way, new colleagues are invited into the community and the culture can be sustained.

4. Find the time, if you possibly can, to go on an occasional retreat in an environment far removed from the school. We are all influenced by context, and it is sometimes difficult to engage in depth with each other in places where interruptions, crises, and the normal hurly-burly of life are just a whisper away. So it can be invaluable to find a peaceful place to gather together for the purposes dealt with in this book.

5. Sometimes assumptions and differences can be surfaced relatively quickly and easily. At other times, more in-depth work is needed. One of the great strengths of Learning to Learn, the leading-edge educational reform effort in South Australia, is that the primary purpose of their learning circles is for leaders to go in depth into the values, beliefs, and assumptions held by the various participants (LeCornu, 2004). The process is strengthened because the facilitators put their own values and assumptions on the line as well.

> These learning circles involve designated school leaders from 6–8 schools/sites coming together twice a term, with Departmental curriculum officers and university colleagues, to reflect on and share their insights, tensions and dilemmas as leaders of the change process, and to grow their understanding of the process. (LeCornu, 2004, p. 1)

This way of proceeding can provide powerful opportunities for professional renewal. But success depends upon almost all the participants having substantial metacognitive skills so that they are adept at looking at themselves.

Classroom as Learning Community

Most of the life of a school takes place in classrooms, and ultimately, classrooms should be authentic learning communities. Yet they often lack the state of relaxed alertness—and the feeling of being a learning community—that makes great learning possible.

The process introduced in this book can help teachers in their classrooms in two ways. First, some of the specific procedures, such as the ordered sharing, can directly help to create the field of listening that supports the optimal state of mind for learning. Second, the state of mind in classrooms and the sense of community are often improved indirectly, just as a result of the ways in which the adults in a school change the ways that they interact and work together. How does that happen?

As the adults work together to improve *their* learning community, they generate a sense of greater well-being through their relationships with each other, with nonteaching staff, and with parents. This affects the school as a whole and filters into many individual classrooms. Remember, for instance, the research on positive affect that we introduced in Chapter 1, which shows that a slight feeling of well-being (which occurs when the adult learning community is flourishing) improves social interactions and verbal fluency in adolescents.

Of course, much more can usually be done in specific ways to improve the learning climate in many classrooms, and that goal can actually be one of the issues PrLCs deal with directly. We discuss our approach to this issue in Chapter 15.

→| |← →| |← →| |← →| |←

Administrative Support

For the PrLC process to succeed, it must have support from leadership. Educators have to deal with an enormous array of often conflicting demands, and the last thing they need is one more program that has to be imposed on staff and ultimately goes nowhere. Here are two points to keep in mind.

First, it helps to begin with the clear knowledge that building the right sort of community does genuinely improve the working lives of teachers and the results they get. For instance, one analysis of 61 Ohio elementary schools led to the following conclusion:

> Students in schools where the staff is working well as a group generally outperform their peers in schools where the staff is not functioning as well. This finding is particularly strong regarding tests of citizenship and across all academic measures for students at high poverty schools. (Laitsch, 2007)

Second, good leaders fight for sufficient resources to make sure that a program can take place. The process learning circles call for at least two meetings a month, each lasting two hours. That time must be found in the work week if teachers are not going to be paid extra for participating. Some schools have made one day a week a shorter day; staff then alternate, dealing with business one week and with this group process the next. Although it is possible to reduce the frequency of meetings a little, say, to once every three weeks, the essential components must be implemented if it is going to produce the results that are sought.

Leadership and the Group Dynamic

We have seen educational leaders display a wide range of attitudes toward programs in the schools and organizations that they lead. Sometimes the leaders denigrate the programs; sometimes they tolerate them; sometimes they support the programs from a distance; sometimes they wholeheartedly and enthusiastically endorse them. That last response is the crucial one.

As a practical matter, any process such as ours leads to the development of shared understandings and ways of functioning together. Participation by leaders is essential for the staff as a whole to develop common understandings about the basis of the process. In Redwood School, for instance (discussed in Chapter 11), the principal was largely absent, but the vice principal was totally committed and a full participant in the process. She proved to be a vital ingredient in the program's success.

At stake is more than just the development of common protocols and ways of working together. A group dynamic is just that—*dynamic*. It is a matter of energy—of enthusiasm and persistence and the sort of attitudes that apply when things are not working well, and ways of celebrating results and supporting each other. All of this and more contribute to the overall energy and vitality of any program.

And leadership is a key. A leader is a spark plug, an inspiration, a source of safety and security, a bearer of the vision, a catalyst for action, a focal point around which individuals and events can gather, a point of coherence as people walk their individual paths.

Great leaders have a combination of competence *and* character, familiarity with the system *and* a center of integrity, management skills *and* the capacity to inspire. One example is the leader of Rose Warren Empowerment School, which we described in Chapter 11. Without a doubt, Rosanna Gallagher is the spark that ignites and sustains the flame that drives her school. Another example is Margot Foster, who has been the leader since the late 1990s of the statewide initiative in South Australia called Learning to Learn. We have been international colleagues of the program for the entire time (it was launched with a workshop on our brain/mind learning principles). Margot has engaged other experts on learning, teaching, building community, complex systems, and more to continually invigorate the program. For the entire period of time she has talked the talk *and* walked the walk.

→| |← →| |← →| |← →| |←

In essence, there is a simple maxim that is critical to success here, just as in every other human endeavor: plan the work, and then work the plan. Following that guideline is how to develop the foundations—the spirit and practice of a powerful learning community—upon which other programs can build.

14

Process Principles

The key to pursuing excellence is to embrace an organic, long-term learning process, and not to live in a shell of static, safe mediocrity.

— *Josh Waitzkin*
(author and chess champion)

As will become clear over time, one key to the success of the process learning circle meetings is an appropriate rhythm and mind-state for communicating and learning. A learning community needs both spontaneity and routine, constancy and becoming, safety and challenge. To that end, here are some process principles that we use as effective guides.

1. Ensure Safety

PrLCs must be psychologically safe so that participants can feel free to genuinely test their own beliefs and assumptions and take risks in publicly exploring their thinking and their practices. This principle has two implications.

First, as we have noted, group participants should usually be volunteers. The best way to sabotage others and ourselves is to force people to be where they do not want to be, and to demand that they change. Such an approach is almost guaranteed to create undue stress.

Second, each participant should make a commitment that nothing personal shared by any other participant will be made public without that person's consent. The consent agreement also says that participants must refrain from commenting on the inner workings of the PrLC on Facebook, Twitter, and other sites. Deciding whether or not to participate in a group is a delicate process. The most basic requirement is trust. In effect, it will take some time for people to decide whether the group can be trusted, and so you should expect to have a few meetings in which people are gauging how safe the group really is.

2. Maintain Consistency

Although the brain/mind loves variety, it must have a degree of routine and consistency. Indeed, it begins to anticipate regular events ahead of time and to prepare for them. This situation can be used to set the stage for your learning and build a good climate in the group.

Preliminaries. Get any venting out of the way. Although the daily pressures of teaching can often be frustrating, the group process should not be used for expressing frustration, which may dilute the energy needed for positive change. We suggest that if the need to vent feelings about the day is strong, then do so briefly before the actual process learning circle begins.

A way to begin. You could start each meeting with a moment, say, one minute, of total and restful silence. Or perhaps begin with some relatively brief relaxation exercise, which might range from stretching to the use of selected music. The process helps to separate what is happening now from the rest of the day, and helps minds and bodies to focus and become present.

A way to end. You may want to close with a simple ceremony. A song is one possibility; a moment of silence is another; a football huddle cheer is a third. For the last option, you stand in a circle (like a huddle in football). The process leader selects a word to say out loud, such as "focus." Together, count out loud "one, two, three." And then clap and say your selected word at the same time. This routine helps to provide the brain/mind with a sense of closure.

3. Maintain the Energy of the Group

The group process is partly about building a field of listening so that people can go deep together. Interruptions hurt the effort. So does nonparticipation. Here are some hints:

• Turn cell phones and beepers off. They are enormously distracting and can totally puncture the atmosphere.

• Unless it is part of the procedure, do not engage in side conversations. In addition to being distracting, side conversations convey a message of disrespect to others and to the group endeavor as a whole.

• Find a balance between talking too softly (which causes others to strain) and talking too loudly, which forces others to back off.

• This is a participative process. Even though some people may prefer to watch and listen more than they talk, silent observers are often a deterrence and an annoyance to others and can lead to a general withholding of energy. This energy can be felt in, say, the difference between a flat experience and a lively one. Everyone needs to actively participate, though the process allows room for a great deal of variation in how much people participate.

• Begin and end roughly on time. Doing so is a way to build coherence and orderliness, and to honor and maintain borders. It also allows people to relax.

4. Stay or Go, but Don't Come and Go

Because the process learning circle is for volunteers, a person should feel free either to participate or not. After the group has begun, a person may wish to drop out, and that is fine. However, once a group has begun or a person has dropped out, membership should be regarded as settled for some definite period, such as a year. This understanding helps the group develop a sense of community, rhythm, and safety, which is almost impossible to do if people come and go.

Geoffrey was cofacilitating a process with about 14 people some years ago. The group included one person who was cheerful and enthusiastic, and completely indifferent to the group's rhythm. She was present at the beginning, did not come to the second meeting, then came to the third and left halfway through after assuring us we were doing good work and encouraging us to continue. She came late to the fourth meeting, sat down, and began to talk. At that point one of the other participants got so fed up that she flatly told the latecomer (we'll call her Evie) to "put up or shut up" because they were all so frustrated with her behavior. This comment was met with vigorous head nodding by almost everyone else. Evie stood up in a huff and walked out. And the rest of the group breathed a huge sigh of relief, relaxed, and quite happily stayed together for the remainder of the program.

Situations like this can be handled in different ways. Sometimes the process leader acts. Sometimes the group acts. But in any event, a decision needs to be made and the participants need to stick with it. If an individual wishes to change her mind, the group should be very cautious about tolerating coming and going. This is not a time to be nice or to try to please or appease people.

5. Slow Down to Speed Up

People often feel a great temptation to "cover" material quickly. That is not the thrust of this process. The reason is grounded in sound learning theory. The goal of the groups is for people to take the time to explore what is important, and to give their brains and minds time to digest what is being considered. This may seem counterintuitive and slow to begin with. In the medium and long term, however, going deep becomes the driving force for significant learning, learning that will actually take less time than if you had tried to hurry it.

This approach can be very difficult to stick to in practice. To help in the effort, one group selected a motto and had it laminated. It was the slogan from *The Hitchhiker's Guide to the Galaxy* and said simply "DON'T PANIC."

6. Recognize That There Are No Initial Outcomes

As the process learning circle format takes participants through the selected material, they will begin to make some mind shifts naturally, and these will be reflected in changes in practice. It is critical for this process that you *not* set out to raise student performance or test scores immediately. Take the time to explore and play with the material that is being worked through. Like anything else, it is important to get your feet wet, and to take the time to develop a feel for the process and for the new strategies and steps that may be tried out in a class.

It is important to feel free and safe enough to take risks and experiment. If you want an immediate, beneficial result, the tendency will be to avoid trying things out altogether or to push too hard.

7. Benefit from Individual Differences

The group will consist of people with different beliefs, goals, styles, roles, and functions. This variety will be immensely valuable in the long run because a wide range of input, attitudes, and ideas will greatly increase your understanding and will be beneficial to you.

However, the differences can also be frustrating. Some people are precise about being on time and following guidelines, and others think that deadlines are meant to be changed and that guidelines are made to be ignored. Both styles (and many others) are important; extremes of all of them are counterproductive.

We therefore suggest that one function of the group process should be to explore individual differences. This exploration will help you to understand each other better, and it will enable you to appreciate and stick to those aspects of the guidelines that really are important to the process that we have developed. It is for this reason that Chapter 12 includes a description of four identity styles, in the form of the Caine Identity Profile. We have been working with the approach for more than 20 years and have applied it to adults and to adolescents. In our experience, understanding identity styles is useful for teachers, for students, *and* for leaders.

8. Do Not Give Each Other Advice Unless Asked

You may be tempted to solve each other's problems. And participants may ask for advice. However, this process is *not* about giving each other advice during PrLC meetings. The goal is for people to learn from their own experience. That is what the search for meaning is all about. So be extremely cautious about giving or asking for advice during the group process as this can frustrate your own learning, even if advice is what you want. Do not ask for it if you don't want it, and stop the process if you don't like the advice. This is a particularly delicate area for process leaders who might want to guide participants in their growth or solve problems for them. In this process it is essential that you create the conditions for people to develop their own awareness and not try to do the learning or solve their problems for them. The process becomes a foundation for self-efficacy.

Note, however, that there is a difference between advice and feedback. Giving gentle and useful feedback is an art, one aspect of which is to be moderately impersonal, so that nothing that is said or received is taken personally. Again, however, feedback needs to be authentically solicited.

9. Honor the Format

Each phase of the group process has a reason and a purpose. The beginnings and endings are clearly noted and need to be adhered to. The reason is that every phase is essential for the deep learning and insights that are needed, but if the various phases are not adhered to, some aspects of the process are inevitably lost.

It may seem that multitasking works and that the various phases can be blended into each other. That can happen in the world *outside* the group process, as people begin to listen to each other more fully and begin to have more compelling professional conversations. But that blending is a consequence of adhering fully to the process so that the various phases become second nature. Every field of expertise requires a mastery of the basics, and that is what the PrLC format allows.

10. Maintain the Process

At times people may feel euphoric. At other times they may feel low. They may even reach a point where nothing seems to be happening or they have strong doubts. Such mood changes are just a part of life. They are also quite natural when we change our mental models. One of the functions of the process learning circles is to develop a feel for continuity of the learning process and for the power of a sense of community, no matter what we are feeling individually. Grasping this can help enormously in your personal learning.

In these situations, it helps to remember the students. They are in school whether they like it or not. They have a great deal to put up with in their personal lives. Their moods may fluctuate. And they also have to learn that things take time. In fact, one of the best ways to benefit from the entire process is to recognize what you are feeling or thinking or experiencing, and then to use that to build empathy with students and others, and to grasp (again) that we are all human.

→| |← →| |← →| |← →| |←

In our experience it helps to have these principles written somewhere and made available to everyone, perhaps as a chart (see Figure 14.1). However, we also know that it takes awhile for the principles to make sense, and this usually happens when one or more have to be called on in dealing with a situation that emerges.

Figure 14.1
Process Principles

1. **Ensure safety.**
   The PrLCs must be psychologically safe.

2. **Maintain consistency.**
   Although the brain/mind loves some variety, it must have a degree of routine and consistency.

3. **Maintain the energy of the group.**
   Develop a field of listening with minimal interruptions.

4. **Stay or go, but don't come and go.**
   Once a group has begun and participation has become firm, membership should usually be regarded as settled for some definite period, such as a year.

5. **Slow down to speed up.**
   The goal of the groups is for people to take the time to explore what is important, and to give their brains and minds time to digest what is being considered.

6. **Recognize that there are no initial outcomes.**
   It is critical for this process to not set out to raise student performance or test scores immediately. Results come as understanding and skill develop.

7. **Benefit from individual differences.**
   Differences are important; extremes are counterproductive.

8. **Do not give each other advice unless asked.**
   This process is not about giving each other advice during PrLC meetings. The goal is for people to learn from their own experience. That is why feedback, appropriately given, can be very useful.

9. **Honor the format.**
   Every phase is essential for the deep learning and insights that are needed.

10. **Maintain the process.**
    Develop a feel for continuity of the learning process and for the power of a sense of community, no matter what you are feeling individually.

15

The Path Forward

Learning is not compulsory... neither is survival.

—W. Edwards Deming

The pressure to perform tends to make all of us think in the short term. Almost all the language and programs currently in play in education reform stress getting results *now*.

Yet at precisely the same time as educators are scrambling to meet the deadlines of the *now*, they need to work toward constant improvement. And the bottom line is that the only way to generate constant improvement is to work in the medium and long term, and to build solid foundations. Quick fixes and solid foundations usually don't mix well.

The PrLCs can be used to deal with specific needs in the relatively short term (say, one year), but sustained success over time calls for a longer view. We have mentioned this point in different ways in this book. For instance, we stress the need to create a healthy learning climate as an essential first step—but that is the beginning and not the end. And we point out that educational leaders need a philosophy of change.

The problem is that a new way of functioning depends upon an appropriate way of thinking. It is not a matter of going where no one has gone before, but of finding thinking tools that guide us in the march toward the future.

This chapter takes for granted the fact that professional development is always a work in progress. It can never end for two reasons. First, the world is changing very rapidly and it is pulling our students with it. Some of the most significant changes include the explosive growth in social networking, the constant expansion of our understanding of how people learn, the tremendous increase in the availability of information—and misinformation—about everything, and radical change in the capacities and availability of technology. Educators have no choice but to adapt constantly. Second, teaching is as demanding as any other profession, including rocket science, and the path from novice to journeyman to expert to master never ends. Becoming a great teacher takes a long time and a lot of work. Here, then, is a way of thinking that we use that emerges out of the research on learning and teaching and that helps to blend the short and the long term. It is based on reframing the core message of standards.

Reframing Goals and Standards

The goal of standards is sustained improvements in student learning. So let us look at standards from the perspective of what makes learning sustainable. This issue applies to every content area without exception, and so we are not addressing specific content here. Rather, the first key is to deal with the differences between surface knowledge and understanding. This is the approach adopted, for instance, in the example in Chapter 10 about improving the teaching of math.

The core challenge—and the primary goal—should be to teach for understanding rather than memorization, but to incorporate memorization when needed. The core problem is that the system, and much of what is being called for in the name of raising standards, leads to teaching for memorization, with minor opportunities for deeper understanding to occur.

Why does this distinction matter? It all has to do with the differences between facts and concepts. The system has reached the point at which, to a large extent, it does not differentiate between facts and concepts, even if the various standards use words like *understand* and *meaningful*.

A concept is an idea that organizes and makes sense of facts. It pulls facts together. It can be used to sift through information. It is a way of thinking. A concept makes it possible for us to generate explanations for ourselves. Thus, if we understand the concept of friction, it is possible to explain why a builder can walk on a slanted roof without falling off, or to use friction as a metaphor to explain and describe the tension between two people who are at odds with each other.

Teaching for understanding means teaching so that students get the underlying concepts. With those as a foundation, facts are easier to remember and advanced levels of understanding become possible. So the indispensable and essential key to raising and sustaining high standards is to consistently teach for understanding. Another way to describe the difference is to distinguish between surface knowledge and what we have called technical/scholastic knowledge (Caine, R., et al., 2008). With that distinction in mind, it becomes possible to plan professional development for the longer term and to select the materials and programs that most suit the needs of a school or a district.

A Path of Professional Development

We have been exploring the many different approaches to professional development for many years. Our reading, research, and experience indicate that there is no need to set different approaches against each other as though one automatically precludes the other. Approaches to instruction follow a path from very simple to very complex, with each mode including but going beyond the one that comes before (Caine, G., & Caine, R., 2008). Here we introduce the first major shift that must be made in order to genuinely raise and sustain high standards—the shift from teaching for memorization to teaching for understanding.

Basic Direct Instruction: Transmission of Information

This form of instruction is based on the view that the primary job of teachers is to transmit what they know, directly or through textbooks, and the primary role of students is to listen or read what is transmitted, respond to teacher questions, and engage in practice and rehearsal. The primary outcome is memorization and shallow understanding—what we call surface knowledge—as revealed on test scores.

Improvement. Most of the programs and procedures currently being used to improve education are geared toward direct instruction, but with widely varying degrees of sophistication. We recommend an initial focus on the following procedures:

- Make teacher presentations more creative, and questioning more insightful.
- Make practice and rehearsal more creative.
- Improve classroom management through methods that emphasize respect and relationship, such as those found in *Discipline with Dignity* (Curwin, Mendler, & Mendler, 2008).
- Loosen the time constraints on testing so that students are not tested every few weeks.
- Provide substantial real-time feedback for students.

Enhanced Direct Instruction: Teaching for Understanding

This form of instruction is based on the view that the primary job of teachers is to help students understand concepts and master core skills, and the primary role of students is to think through material, solve problems, ask questions, and come to understand material by working on and with it in practical ways. The primary outcome is understanding and skill, as reflected in a variety of authentic ways of performing and demonstrating understanding and skill, supplemented by test scores.

Improvement. Some very powerful materials and programs are available for helping teachers function at this level. They range from the use of Socratic questioning, through the Annenberg Media Program on the Learning Classroom, to the ASCD program on teaching the Whole Child. More specifically, teachers can learn how to do the following:

- Encourage students to ask and find answers to their own questions.
- Enhance the ways in which students can communicate with each other and work together.
- Create meaningful problems and projects.
- Ask sophisticated questions that help students reflect on and process their work.
- Use more complex modes of formative and summative assessment, including portfolios, products, and presentations.

Practical Implications

When we look at instruction from this perspective, some of the invisible problems of professional development become visible, including the following:

- Some teachers and administrators are more sophisticated than others, and so a particular program may help some while hindering others. The key is to see what aspect of professional development a program is targeting and to work with teachers to discern their next best steps.
- The more sophisticated the approach to instruction, the more complex assessment needs to be. Specifically, anything beyond a transmission model of teaching calls for a combination of authentic assessment and appropriate testing.
- It will become apparent that sometimes it is system constraints that limit the development that is possible. For instance, good project-based education really needs longer blocks of time than periods of 45 or 50 minutes. And good professional development requires that educators have enough available time.

• A core message should be that the way to improve test scores is not to engage in a great deal of test preparation, but to improve the sophistication of the teaching. Higher test scores follow.

And There's More

The shift from teaching for memorization to teaching for understanding is the first and most important shift for education to make. But it is not the last step to take, as many readers will know. Both of the instructional approaches described earlier are still very much teacher directed, and even the second does not fully prepare students for life in the real world.

Our research indicates that in addition to memorization and deep understanding is a third type of knowledge, which we call dynamical or performance knowledge. It is the capacity to use what has been studied in the real world in unplanned as well as planned situations. Acquiring that type of knowledge requires a further shift in instruction. We call this third approach the "guided experience approach." Here, student interests and questions drive the process, and learning involves immersion in real-world contexts where the standards are lived and experienced interactively. Teaching in this way is very sophisticated and should, we believe, be a long-term goal for education. However, it is beyond the scope of this book. For those who wish to pursue the issue, we address it in two books. *Making Connections: Natural Learning, Technology, and the Human Brain* (2011) spells out the theoretical foundation and provides an overview of the model. And *Seeing Education in a New Light* (2011) details in depth the differences between the three instructional approaches and the worldviews or perceptual orientations that underlie them.

Technology: The Gateway to the Future

This book is a traditional way of communicating, and the sorts of communities that it focuses on involve people meeting face-to-face in the real world, in real time. But, as we noted in Chapter 1, that world is changing rapidly. And, with some exceptions, education simply has not come to grips with the emerging reality. For instance, online social networking means that millions of people are interacting very quickly, in both private and public ways, irrespective of distance, and on almost every conceivable topic. In addition, huge amounts of information, and numerous expressions of opinion, are available everywhere just by maneuvering a mouse or touching a screen—except in most schools, where even staff are severely restricted in their access to e-mail and the Web. And for those whose only e-mail address is through a school system, that access is severely limited after hours as well.

And yet we must prepare for and enter that world.

With that end in mind, the need to focus on and master teaching for understanding is even more important. Although technology is awash with the transmission of information, the way in which technology works best, and the direction toward which it is pointing, is beyond a transmission model of teaching. Students will be exposed over time to videos, webcasts, interactive projects, online groups, conflicting opinions, multiple sources of information (some strong and some weak), unprecedented peer pressure, a blend of information and entertainment, video and online gaming, and networking of multiple kinds. For instance, the Kaiser Family Foundation report *Generation M2* (Rideout, Foehr, & Roberts, 2010) shows that children between the ages of 8 and 18 spend, on average, 53 hours a week with media of different sorts.

As a way of becoming more familiar with the world of technology, it could be introduced into the PrLC process. For instance, both for your own convenience and to become familiar with the worlds that your students will inhabit, we suggest that you experiment with PrLCs that are partially online. This approach frees up participants to connect at nighttime or on weekends as well as during the week. It removes many of the constraints of time and space. And, depending on the software and platforms used, a wide range of resources becomes available that can be shared at a distance, ranging from videos and slideshows, to coediting text and writing notes on virtual whiteboards. Although some protocols, such as the ordered sharing, obviously cannot be followed in the same way, others can work. One example is the use of meeting-room software that allows participants to "raise their hands" to speak. Clearly, much of the relationship derived from physical interactions is lost. That is why we much prefer to conduct most of the PrLCs in the physical world. The virtual world, however, is rushing toward us all. It will shape education of the future, and we need to be prepared.

Much is happening in the world of education, and immense possibilities are opening up for personal and professional expansion. We hope that the process unpacked in these pages will help you to sort through and organize that cornucopia of available material so as to reduce the feelings of being overwhelmed and to harness the joy of being an educator.

Appendix A

How People Learn

The goal of our process of professional development is for participants to improve their everyday, real-world performance. What matters is how teachers function in classrooms and when interacting with students, and what administrators and others do in the course of their everyday work. This requires more than intellectual understanding or doing something effectively in a workshop or an inservice session.

For this goal to be met, the place to begin is with a basic understanding of how people learn naturally, because natural learning is the way in which all people at all times in the history of the human race have come to improve their performance in the real world. We have been researching natural learning for the last 20 years. Most of our books are included in the references, and an overview of our findings can be found on two websites: www.cainelearning.com and www.naturallearninginstitute.org. This appendix offers a simple introduction to how people learn naturally.

The Dance Between Perception and Action

The essence of natural learning is the engagement of perception and action. All real-world learning does two things. First, it changes the way that people come to see and interpret things, situations, and themselves—that is, how and what they perceive. In other words, people develop different ways to "read" the world. Infants are doing this all the time. And so is anyone who immigrates to a new country or becomes highly skilled in some profession, such as interior design or neuroscience or politics. Second (and this happens in parallel), people also develop new ways of acting. They acquire new and additional skills. One way to observe this development is to follow the path of someone mastering a sport—say, beginning with shooting hoops in a driveway to becoming a star in basketball.

When biologists and scientists describe the process of coming to see and act in a new way, they are actually describing progress in terms of perception-action cycles. These cycles recur throughout life because people are always testing and either confirming or changing how they perceive and act. It is a natural capacity that we all have and that we all use to interact with our world (Caine, R., & Caine, G., 2011). Although the overall process is complex, in principle it is very simple: people observe, act, get feedback, and do or do not change. This simple diagram illustrates the process:

Perception <——> Action <——> Feedback <——> New Learning

The key is to learn from the feedback.

A good example is the process of becoming a seasoned teacher or administrator. New teachers can be nervous when they begin a first job, even if they have interned previously. It is possible to be daunted by student behavior, fooled by the games that people play, uncertain about lessons, and more. With experience, a settling down occurs—the patterns of student behaviors become clear, the ways in which a particular school functions become familiar, interactions with parents and the community begin to fall into place. And then there is the ongoing process of professional development—some people follow a clear growth path; others simply bide their time as fads come and go. From the perspective of perception and action, none of this is right or wrong. It's all part of the process. The point is that new teachers are constantly immersed in a sea of experience, read events the best way that they can and act accordingly, are constantly bombarded with feedback, and so adapt and adjust and "learn" to see and act in particular ways. Life is like that.

Engaging Every Aspect of Body, Brain, and Mind

Science is now explaining what everyday life has confirmed over centuries. Natural learning is not just an intellectual process. Both perceptual change and skill development for real-world performance involve the interactive working of all the different features of a human being.

The central notion is that each person is an integrated living system (Damasio, 1999; Fuster, 2003). That means that body, brain, heart, and mind are all involved in learning.

Note that there are many different views of the relationship among body, brain, and mind; and between mind and consciousness. Some scientists and philosophers who are materialists, in that they believe that only material things are real, argue that mind and consciousness are illusions and that the brain is all that there is. At the other end of the spectrum are scientists and philosophers who argue that mind is the foundation of reality. And there are many views that fall somewhere in the middle. For instance, the philosopher John Searle is a materialist who believes that mind and brain are different but that both are real. (See, e.g., a video interview with him at http://www.closertotruth.com/video-profile/Can-Brain-Explain-Mind-John-Searle-/158.) For introductory purposes, we distinguish among brain, mind, and body as follows:

• The body is the entire physical structure;
• The brain is the physical machinery of cognition, where cognition includes sensory and emotional responses;
• The mind is a type of energy that incorporates the totality of subjective experience.

In practice, all three interact, which is why definition is so difficult.

Our approach, therefore, has been to synthesize research across many disciplines, dealing with body, brain, and mind, ranging from neuroscience to cognitive psychology. Our goal has been to develop a set of useful and accurate principles that describe how the brain/mind learns. We used to call this approach brain-based learning and now describe it as natural learning (Caine, R., & Caine, G., 1991, 1994, 2011). We have spelled this out in depth in terms of a set of 12 principles of natural learning with the supporting research (Caine, G., & Caine, R., 2001, 2008; Caine, R., & Caine, G., 1991; 1994).

In our view, such principles need to meet the following four basic criteria:

• *The phenomena described by a principle should be universal.* A brain/mind learning principle must be true for all human beings, despite individual genetic variations, unique experiences, and developmental differences.

• *Research documenting any specific principle should span more than one field or discipline.* Because a learning principle describes a system's property, one would expect validation and confirmation from research across multiple fields and disciplines.

• *A principle should anticipate future research.* It should be expected that emerging research will refine and confirm each principle. For example, much of the brain research on the links between emotion and cognition was published after we first formulated our principles (Caine, R., & Caine, G., 1990).

• *The principle should provide implications for practice.* Learning principles should, as a minimum, provide the basis for an effective general framework to guide decisions about teaching and training, and help in the identification and selection of appropriate methods and strategies.

The Brain/Mind Principles of Natural Learning

One way to benefit from our brain/mind principles is to see that each one reveals capacities for learning, and steps to take, that apply to everyone. So one key to enhancing learning is to capitalize on those capacities. The following list of principles includes suggestions for how to do so.

1. *All learning is physiological.* The brain changes as a result of experience, a phenomenon known as neural plasticity. And the body

changes as well. So new learning is literally structured in our physiology. This is sometimes called "embodied cognition" (Lakoff & Johnson, 1999; Thompson, 2007; Varela, Thompson, & Rosch, 1991).

Implication: Students and staff need adequate sensory engagement, physical movement, and action. Sitting still all the time is tiring, boring, and counterproductive. Students and staff also need to take some action to implement what they study. This can take any form from role playing or making presentations to working on substantial projects that incorporate some of the standards. This applies both to skills and to abstract ideas and concepts.

2. *The brain/mind is social.* We are all born with what Brothers (1997) called the "contact urge." Recent research on mirror neurons confirms that the social nature of human beings is grounded in biology (Rizzolatti et al., 2008). So the brain/mind is designed to learn by imitation and from modeling. The social nature of learning is sometimes described in terms of situated learning (see, e.g., Lave & Wenger, 1991). And Goleman (2007) talks of social intelligence.

Implication: It is important for students of all ages to have opportunities to sit with, talk to, and work with each other. So create communities of practice (Wenger et al., 2002) and opportunities to introduce material through informal conversations between friends, colleagues, and others. In addition, ensure that learners see and experience the new material being used appropriately and naturally.

3. *The search for meaning is innate.* We all have what has been called "an explanatory drive" (Gopnik et al., 1999). In practice, this means that we tend to filter input, organize information and experience, and ask questions according to what we are interested in and care about. And at a deep level we have a hunger for meaningfulness and purpose (Frankl, 2006; Hillman, 1996).

Implication: Find ways to relate new information and practices to authentic learner interests, questions, purposes, ideas, and passions. And find ways to honor and acknowledge authentic student and staff questions and decision making in their learning.

4. *The search for meaning occurs through patterning.* The brain and mind naturally extract patterns from, and impose patterns on, reality (Restak, 1995). So meaning is grounded in how things are connected with each other. Cognitive psychologists use many different terms to describe these patterns, such as *categories, frames,* and *schemata.*

Implication: Find ways to help learners make connections by way of metaphor, identifying common phases, asking questions, making observations, and discovering links to what is already known. Also use projects and problems that naturally organize information and experience in ways that make sense. Service learning does this well.

5. *Emotions are critical to patterning.* Cognition and emotion interact. Neuroscience now shows that emotions are involved in every thought, decision, and response (Damasio, 1999; Pert, 1997). Powerful learning is enhanced by rich emotional experiences, guided and moderated by higher-order functions. In fact, emotion and physical reactions are so much a part of understanding (and comprehending text) that psychologist Eugene Gendlin (1982) describes the link in terms of the phrase "felt meaning." And neuroscientist Antonio Damasio (1999) talks of "the feeling of what happens." This means that the way a person feels about an idea or a skill always influences how well it is understood or mastered. (See Roald, 2008, for a thorough discussion.)

Implication: Introduce new material in ways that are inviting, and make it possible for learners to establish a genuinely positive emotional link to that material.

6. *The brain/mind processes parts and wholes simultaneously.* The brain has modules for discerning specific and separate features of reality. There is also a constant ongoing synthesis of experience at different levels of a hierarchy, culminating in the prefrontal cortex, sometimes called the integrative cortex (Fuster, 2003). Gestalt psychology (Sternberg, 2008) explicitly shows how the mind connects parts to make these wholes. And some of the most recent brain research is now exploring this relationship between parts and wholes in terms of neural networks—lattices of individual neurons

that fire together (Fuster, 2003; Greene, 2010). This means that every skill and concept is better understood and mastered when an interplay occurs between the specific elements and the concept or skill as a whole.

Implication: Introduce and organize new material in terms of natural wholes such as projects, stories, and big ideas.

7. *Learning involves both focused attention and peripheral perception.* Everyone is continuously immersed in a field of stimuli and constantly selects a part of that field to attend to. Attention is a natural phenomenon guided by interest, novelty, emotion, and meaning, and paying attention is critical. In addition, human beings also learn from the background—the context that is not consciously attended to. This reality is illustrated by research on implicit memory (Schacter, 1996) and on mirror neurons (Rizzolatti et al., 2008), which shows how children "pick up" behaviors, beliefs, and preferences or dislikes while engaging in life experience. Claxton (1999) describes this as "learning by osmosis."

Implication: In addition to finding ways to help learners stay engaged, design the physical context so that it indirectly conveys information, connections, and suggestions that support what is being learned.

8. *Learning is both conscious and unconscious.* In addition to intentionally trying to make sense of things and master them, the brain/mind also processes information and experiences below the level of awareness. This can be called the cognitive unconscious (see, e.g., Lakoff & Johnson, 1999; Kihlstrom, 2007). Beyond that, really successful self-regulators are also capable of monitoring themselves by means of the executive functions of their brains (Denkla, 1999) so that they know their own strengths and weaknesses and can take charge of how they process text.

Implication: Incorporate processes, such as the arts, that prime unconscious incubation. And help learners develop their metacognitive capacities so that they become more conscious of, and take better charge of, the ways in which they process and digest experience.

9. *There are at least two types of memory.* Scientists have identified several different memory systems (Schacter, 1996). However, all the different memory systems interact in everyday experience (Fuster, 2003) as more complex networks are created (see Greene, 2010). One key practical distinction is between systems that are used to archive and store information and routines (sometimes by rote memory), and systems that naturally register, make sense of, and store ongoing experience.

Implication: Use projects, stories, situations, and problems that organize material into experiences that are naturally remembered. Assist students of all ages to use in-depth observation and analysis of what transpires, and guide them to deeper understanding by ongoing and effective questioning. Guide them through mindful practice, such as editing and reediting their writing. Memorization techniques, such as creative practice and rehearsal, can then be employed occasionally and as needed.

10. *Learning is developmental.* Development has at least two different dimensions. The first concerns the development of identity and general capacities, such as the shift from concrete to abstract thinking. The second is a rough progression in the mastery of a discipline, from novice to expert. (See, generally, Ericsson, Charness, Feltovich, & Hoffman, 2006.)

Implication: Professional development, and learning in the classroom, should be scaffolded to take into consideration both the capacities of the learners and their current state of knowledge and competence. And many opportunities should be available to reflect on experience and to deal with regular feedback, so that insight and understanding can develop over time.

11. *Complex learning is enhanced by challenge and inhibited by threat associated with helplessness and/or fatigue.* A great deal of research shows that effective mental functioning can be sabotaged by fears associated with helplessness. The brain/mind literally becomes less effective and people lose access to their own capacities for higher-order functioning and creativity when the survival response kicks

in. As we show in Chapter 1, LeDoux (1996) calls this response the "low road." And Olsen and Sexton (2009) call it "threat rigidity." It is triggered by such factors as being overwhelmed, losing control, experiencing excessive stress, and meaninglessness.

Implication: Establish good relationships within a classroom or other environment so that adults and students, learners and leaders listen to each other, and students feel safe to ask questions, make suggestions, and try things out. Use projects and processes that make sense, and allow students to pursue their own interests within the context of the projects. And ensure that students have adequate resources and some control over the use of their time and how they will proceed.

12. *Each brain is uniquely organized.* Although all people have many capacities and qualities in common, everyone is also a unique blend of experience and genetics. Many ways of identifying individual differences are available. A good example is Gardner's theory of multiple intelligences (1993). Another is the Myers-Briggs personality typology. We have developed our own identity styles profile by synthesizing many of the other options available (see Chapter 12). And in addition to individual differences are social and cultural differences that affect how people learn.

Implication: Professional development, and classroom learning, must be designed so that it both treats everyone equally and at the same time helps individuals to capitalize on their own strengths. It helps to use a good learning-style inventory so that participants can grasp some of their own predispositions and preferences. And educators need to develop an awareness of different cultures and customs.

The Goal of Professional Development Revisited

Natural learning is a cradle-to-grave biologically based process, through which every human being comes to know how to function in the real world. Infants use it, and people who become expert in anything have to use it as well.

Our goal is to support professional development that helps educators develop real-world competence—performance knowledge—that is genuinely learner centered and that calls for very high standards. The task is to make natural learning useful and practical. In effect, educators need to be able to effectively and naturally perceive—read—students, standards, their colleagues, the school, and themselves.

Appendix B

The Field of Listening

The secret of strength lies in the quiet mind.
—White Eagle, The Quiet Mind

As we write in Chapter 2, one of the core ingredients in building community and a sense of safety and commitment is for the participants to feel heard. Here we consider the obvious corollary—listening.

Layers of Listening

There are many different ways to listen and various layers of listening. One way to describe them is in terms of a range from the relatively shallow to the relatively deep.

Listening at the Surface

Have you ever interacted with people in a situation in which listening tends to be perfunctory and superficial? An easy way to test for that is to simply observe the extent to which you (or others) feel or do the following:

• Assume that you know what a speaker is going to say before she has finished speaking.

• Jump in with an opinion before a person has finished speaking.

• Have no pauses in a conversation.

• Assume that someone has nothing useful to contribute.

• Speak without paying attention to what others in the group are actually interested in.

• Talk across each other.

All of these are quite natural aspects of communication. They occur during casual chats, heated conversations, arguments, and sharing of experiences. And several interactions are actually going on. Sometimes people are dealing with content intellectually; sometimes they appear to be talking about content but are actually maintaining social relationships; sometimes they may be competing with each other with words as weapons; and sometimes they are really bored and are just keeping up appearances. So all sorts of things are happening. And although the listening fluctuates in intensity and people sometimes actually do feel heard, they can just as easily feel excluded.

Intentional, Active Listening

A more intentional type of listening is slower and more courteous. It occurs when we listen for the purpose of understanding or learning something new, or are really trying to help each other or to work with each other. Think for a moment about times when you have had this experience. What happened, and how would you characterize this type of listening?

In our experience, this mode involves patterns of behavior that differ from the superficial mode in the following ways:

• There tends to be time for questions.
• The conversation may include momentary pauses.
• A more gentle give and take occurs, as ideas are probed or situations are examined.

Of course, this is not always the case, but it is what tends to emerge.

The use of active listening (Gordon, 2003) usually promotes the creation of this space. It is a structured way of listening and responding in which people pay attention to words, body language, and feelings, and work at suspending their own frames of reference and judgments. People work at listening, at clarifying what is being said and sought. And precisely because real listening takes place, the process is used for such purposes as conflict resolution, management, counseling, and journalism.

Deep Listening

Have you ever heard others, and felt heard, so fully that you knew there was no need to have to defend yourself, or compete for time, or feel anxious about being judged? And you actively enjoyed the presence of those with whom you were communicating? And disagreements were simply steps along the way to a deeper understanding?

These are indicators of a type of listening that is deeper than active listening. Although it does involve a type of discipline, it is less intellectually effortful than active listening. It is a little difficult to describe the experience accurately, because it is as much about noticing as listening. It fully engages the body, the mind, and the heart—so that everything about a person participates. And it is a space within which it becomes much easier to notice our own deep habits and beliefs and to begin to become less attached to them. So deep listening naturally involves listening to ourselves as well as to the others with whom we are engaged.

One of the best and most well known paths of deep listening is dialogue. As we have written elsewhere:

Dialogue is *not* debate and argument (with winners and losers). It is not consensus building (where agreement is reached but underlying beliefs are unchanged). It is *not* sensitivity training (where "we" become sensitive to "them"). It is *not* discussion (which is an exploration and a breaking apart of ideas without going beyond intellectual analysis). All of these have a place and a role....

[Dialogue is different. Dialogue] is a process in which participants in a group gradually begin to shed masks, roles, and fixed ideas so that they can penetrate deeper meanings and come together in a genuine sense of communion. There is no competition for space or time, and everyone knows that he will have an adequate opportunity to speak and be heard. (Caine, R., & Caine, G., 1997a, p. 144)

A current approach to dialogue was initiated and driven by David Bohm (1996), one of the world's great physicists. He did not invent it, but he established dialogue as a useful and powerful process and provided many of the core principles in vogue today. *Dialogue* means "the flow of meaning," and Bohm took that notion seriously. He showed that it is possible for groups to get beneath the literal meaning of words and get a handle on what is really being said and intended and felt. A nonverbal field of meaning exists in which people can hold differences without dissonance.

The practice may seem peculiar at first. For example, participants usually sit in a circle. They may use a talking stick (an old tradition that is still used extensively) because it ensures that the only person who is talking is the one holding the stick. This method puts a damper on interruptions. Each individual is free to talk about whatever is on his mind, so there is no necessary flow of discussion about a particular topic. And participants share a clear understanding that no one is going to be held to what he has said, so that the process builds in an openness to changing one's mind by suspending beliefs and withholding premature judgments.

The process of dialogue is more sophisticated than we have described here, but we have provided enough to show that it is radically different from most discussion and debate, and all the phases allow for a different flow of communication and a different depth of listening. The process has been found to be invaluable in the hard-nosed worlds of business and management (see, e.g., Isaacs, 1999).

Many others have created and developed ways for inviting and encouraging people to communicate and listen at deeper levels than is found in everyday life. Here are some examples:

• *Turning to one another through conversation*—In her book *Turning to One Another*, Margaret Wheatley (2009) develops the theme that one of the most important ways to deal with challenging circumstances in any context is to begin conversations about things that are important to you and those near you.

• *The art of hosting* (http://www.artofhosting.org/home/)—Toke Paludan Moeller and his colleagues have developed an elegant process that integrates dialogue and other processes with advanced notions of complex systems that show how to acknowledge and work with chaos and turbulence in groups dealing with difficult issues, on the way to finding deeper collective meanings and innovative solutions.

• *The world café* (http://www.theworldcafe.com/)—Created by Juanita Brown, the world café is a process in which many people, often numbering in the many hundreds, are seated in small groups with a guided process for exploring some issue. Membership in groups then rotates. Over time, many people interact in these small groups and some wonderful insights often emerge.

• *The sacred art of listening* (http://www.sacredlistening.com; Lindahl & Schnapper, 2002)— The thrust of this approach is for people to learn to listen from the heart, and in so doing enrich relationships and rekindle a spiritual path.

The Field of Listening

The field of listening combines active listening with deep listening. It is a relaxed space of intentional and exploratory engagement, where it is OK to express personal opinions and to change one's mind immediately, and where there is no competition for time and yet participants sense that everyone will have an opportunity to share and will also feel heard.

Sometimes the field emerges quite naturally, particularly if a conversation is led by someone who does actually listen in these ways. In general, however, specific processes are needed to generate the field. The goal, then, is to initiate and sustain this field throughout a school or district so that it naturally becomes part of the way in which people connect to and interact with each other.

As a practical matter, this philosophy has a profound effect in the classroom. As educators build a field of listening with each other, they carry that attitude into the classroom. It then becomes easier to listen to students, and to help students listen to each other. And the very fact of being heard tends to increase motivation, a sense of ownership, and participation.

The field of listening shows up in teacher dialogue. Teachers' comments reveal shifts in the ways that they listen to each other. Here is the comment of one teacher after she had experienced one aspect of our process (the ordered sharing) for the first time:

> [Very enthusiastic] I find as teachers we are so passionate . . . we disagree or believe wholeheartedly, and we go "yes . . . no . . . uh . . ." and we butt in [laughing], and it's hard to get your ideas out or to listen fully to someone else's ideas, so to just go around and be forced to listen . . . [slowing down] it's kind of . . . it brings your . . . it's more peaceful [more gentle laugh].

Of course, the goal is to shift the ways in which teachers and administrators listen to and interact with each other generally over time, and not just as a response to a process in a workshop. Here are two responses from teachers two months into a yearlong program using our process (described in Chapter 11):

> I truly feel like a professional because we find ourselves talking about learning and what we are doing with students.

> With my colleagues, we have begun listening to each other more quietly and carefully in meetings (I'm still working on it).

Listening and Process Learning Circles

The process learning circle format has been developed over a period of about 30 years. It is grounded in procedures that Geoffrey first encountered in the 1970s and has been nourished by many of the ideas and procedures described here, as well as by the experiences we have had with the process in our work with schools and other organizations.

One phase of the format, the ordered sharing, specifically sets the stage for listening, and it anchors the process learning circle. As described elsewhere in this book, however, the process has four essential phases. Each of these can be used separately, but when they are used together appropriately, a wonderful field of listening emerges over time.

Appendix C

The Second Meeting
of Spring Valley's PrLC

The PrLC has met a first time, and the four phases of that meeting, as well as other aspects of the process, are described at the end of Chapters 4 through 9. Here we depict the second meeting, which takes place in the middle of the month.

This meeting features the same four phases of the process learning circle, but the focus is different than that of the first meeting. Although the rhythm of the overall procedure is maintained, this meeting is largely a practical discussion about the experiences that the participants had, what they learned, and how they plan to proceed for the rest of the month.

1. Ordered Sharing

Each participant will share *briefly* about what was attempted and something about what happened.

> *Camille*: I decided to change the seating in my room, and the first time I did it I totally lost control when they were in groups. So I had to set up a way to get their attention. But when they worked on the math problems together, the energy was amazing. They love it! I noticed this because when I walked around they were totally engrossed and simply ignored me most of the time.
>
> *Jayson*: Some of the teams doing joint assignments really worked well together, but others just did their own stuff even when they

were in pairs. You could see some of them just ignoring others. Then I changed it and told them to select their own assignments. That worked beautifully, except that there were always a couple taking charge and not giving the others time. I've got to find a way to fine-tune this.

[Other participants describe their experiences.]

2. Reflective Study

The reflective study now becomes reflection on action. One way to do this is to form triads. Each participant will have about 5 minutes to describe in more detail what happened with the action taken. Then the two others in the triad will spend the next 10 minutes asking questions and helping the first participant spell out in more detail what was attempted, what happened, how what was happening was evident, and what insights were gained.

After about 15 minutes, the second participant in each triad has the opportunity to describe the experimental action taken. And then the third has a turn.

Note that in every instance, it is important to keep a two-pronged focus—dealing with what happened specifically and also referring back to the topic of the material being explored. In this case, the material is about the social nature of the brain/mind and how that affects learning.

Example 1

Camille: As I said, there was no problem sometimes when they were going at the math problems. But other times when the desks were arranged in groups, some of the students just got caught up in their own conversations. It was really difficult to get their attention when I needed to.

Q: Was there any configuration that worked better than the others?

Camille: Well, now that I think about it, there was no problem if most of the kids in the groups were looking at me.

Q: Have you ever helped them learn how to listen to each other? I use the ordered sharing with mine, and it really helps.

Camille: Now, that's an interesting idea. You mean that if they practice the ordered sharing they might pay more attention to each other and to me at other times? I think I'll try that.

Process leader [listening in]: Isn't it interesting how the group just took over. Why do you think that happened?

Camille: They were interested in their own stuff, weren't they? I guess groups are driven by what they care about.

Process leader: Perhaps they need to see better behavior modeled so that their mirror neurons can kick in to help you. How might you do that?

Camille: Hmm... I've got to think about that. [To others] What do you guys think?

[Discussion]

Example 2

Jayson: Well, I definitely need to look at what to do with the groups when a couple of students take charge of everything.

Q: The first question that occurs to me is why you think equal participation is important. Aren't the others learning from the ones who take charge?

Jayson: I guess there might be a type of learning, but I've finally come to believe that kids have got to do it if they are going to understand. Seems to me that they should all be asking questions and solving problems and making things happen. I think that's what social learning is really all about. Do you read it differently?

Q: No. I agree with you. I was just testing [laughter]. It's pretty clear that there are natural leaders, but everyone needs to be doing stuff.

Q: I remember that Camille talked about having the kids do the ordered sharing. Would that help you?

Jayson: It might. They have to learn how to listen to each other. But I think that there's something else happening.

Q: You mentioned natural leaders. Remember that we took that inventory about identity styles. Could it be that if they knew more about learning styles that would help the groups function better?

Jayson: You know, that's a thought... [getting excited]... Of course! The social stuff is real. They're all trying to make their mark and fit in and connect.

Q: And those mirror neurons are firing. I wonder who is imitating whom? So what do you think you might do next?

Jayson: I think I need to go back and read the stuff on social learning that we covered last time. And then I want to get my hands on something that shows how people are different—I think that learning styles fits in well here. I bet that they would love to find out about how they are alike and how they are different.

Process leader: You know, we're going to do some stuff on individual differences in a few months. I've got some of that material if you want to jump into it now. If it works for you, you might even be willing to lead part of the process circle when we get to that.

Jayson: This could get interesting!

If time is sufficient, this reflective study phase can be done in the group as a whole, and both the process leader and other participants can ask clarifying questions and, when appropriate, introduce ideas and suggestions. Although working in the group as a whole is time-consuming, it can also be immensely helpful to expand the range of actions that the participants hear about and think about.

Sometimes the first two or three discussions consume a lot of time. It would then be appropriate to divide into smaller groups for the rest of the session so that everyone has an opportunity to be heard.

3. Further Commitment to Action

On the basis of the insights gained during the meeting, each participant revises the action to take for the rest of the month. Some will continue in precisely the same way. Some will modify their actions a little. Some may choose to do something quite different. In every case, the goal is to stick with the same general idea—in this case, the social nature of learning—and to apply it in a personal and practical way that can subsequently be studied.

In our example, both Camille and Jayson have developed a sense of what they want to do next. They would use this time to spell out specific action steps to which they then commit.

4. Regrouping

This phase usually takes the form of an ordered sharing. The participants individually share the essence of what they are taking away with them from this meeting, and what they intend to focus on in the next two weeks.

Sasha: The thing that stood out for me today is that some of the processes that we use, like the ordered sharing, can also be used with the kids. I guess that means that *everything* that we do could be used in my class. That's got me really thinking.

Camille: I love the way that we worked through everything together. The idea that I got about using the ordered sharing is so obvious, and yet I might never have thought about it. Pooling ideas works!

Dore: The thing that blows me away is that *we* are demonstrating social learning in action. We're doing it. It's making sense in a way that I just didn't get before.

Ramona: I want more research on how this works. Remember when we looked at "situated cognition"? That means that the context and the setting matter a lot. I want to know more because I'm getting that my classroom is like a real society, with all sorts of social things happening that affect learning. Any of you guys want to work with me on that?... [laughing and turning to the process leader]... I know, I know. We'll talk about that after this sharing is over. Relationship is just so important to them as well as to us.

[Others add their comments.]

Logistics

The process leader now leads a very brief discussion, because a decision has to be made. It may be that the group should spend another month on the same material. Or it may be that a new topic is selected for the next month. In either case, after any necessary discussion the process leader announces the time and place for the next meeting, and what the topic will be.

Some action is taken to bring the meeting to a close. Perhaps clapping hands, as occurs after a football huddle. Perhaps a brief moment of silence.

Soon after, the process leader will plan a brief experience for the next meeting to lead the participants into the reflective study and will ensure that all reading materials are available.

Appendix D

Expanding Online

As this is being written, e-mail messages are coming in. A few are from online groups in which I (Geoffrey) participate. One is a Yahoo group on small schools. Another is from a professional networking group on LinkedIn. A third shows me that someone wants to be a "friend" on Facebook. I've just browsed the blog entries on Rethink Learning Now, which is a dynamic partnership of those seeking to influence the reauthorization of the *Elementary and Secondary Education Act* (the birthplace of *No Child Left Behind*). Last night I listened to a webinar (along with 35,000 others from around the world) on evolutionary spirituality (much to my disgust, I fell asleep). Yesterday afternoon Renate conducted a meeting with a group of colleagues interested in a new high school. They were sitting in a circle in our office, with one attendee "sitting in" using a laptop computer and communicating from Las Vegas via Skype and his webcam. And next week I plan to participate in a webinar with Kay Lindahl because I am really curious about improving the ways in which people listen to each other online.

All this is but a taste of what can be done with the technologies that are now available, when people want to learn from and with each other, or work together, or conduct campaigns, or build community.

An Introduction to Online Tools to Enrich Professional Learning Communities

A vast array of tools is available to educators—unless, of course, they are blocked by district firewalls! Remember, however, that the online world is turbulent. Some services vanish in the blink of an eye. Meanwhile, others emerge that weren't even thought of a year earlier. So even the introductory resources mentioned here may have changed drastically by the time you read this book.

Conference Calls

You can arrange free conference calls in a number of ways, either by phone or online. Just do an online search for "free conference calls." Conference calls enable large numbers of people to be on a call together. However, no one can see anyone else, and finding the "right" way to jump in and participate is often difficult and frustrating. It helps to have one person facilitate those conversations, but the facilitator's tools will be limited because there is no way to indicate a desire to participate other than by just talking.

Discussion Groups

Many ways of forming interest groups are available, with the opportunity to keep them closed or to open them to others. Yahoo groups and Google groups are good places to start. Each of these also already hosts many thousands of interest groups that may relate to your issues and conversations.

Video Conferencing

Two-way video conferencing is available for free from several sources. Current examples are Skype and ooVoo. Peer coaches can use this method to talk after school and on weekends. It is also relatively inexpensive to arrange for up to six people to participate in videoconferences, and we expect this capacity to increase substantially very quickly. This option can be helpful for those who want to meet and continue a discussion about any topic. Participants can see each other, but it is still important to establish some protocols for how to interact and to have a process leader who facilitates the conversation.

Websites and Blogs

Some services allow participants to read documents, jointly edit documents, watch videos on YouTube, and talk at the same time. This means that a PrLC can accumulate many resources and references and store them in a central place to which all participants have access at any time. In addition, Google and other companies offer individuals the opportunity to create their own websites and blogs for free. Websites tend to be places where people display materials of different sorts. Wikis are websites that can be edited jointly. Wikis and personal websites can be invaluable to teachers in PrLCs who can compile resources and display their work in different ways. Blogs are vehicles for the expression of personal opinions and for interacting with others who want to comment on those opinions. For those who want to explain in more depth what they are doing and what they are thinking, blogs often do the trick.

Cautions and Red Flags

The use of these and other technologies can hurt as well as help. That is why we recommend that they be discussed in the PrLC before being implemented and that basic protocols be established. This is sometimes called "netiquette."

Safety and Privacy

A fundamental feature of the PrLCs is the emphasis on safety and privacy. People listen to and respect each other when they meet, and they do *not* disclose to others what transpires in the meetings. This understanding is essential for the creation of an atmosphere in which participants willingly and publicly talk about their own learnings and the issues with which they are dealing. That is why we have not added social networking to the list of useful technologies. Facebook, Twitter, and other services are largely open. It is simply wrong for PrLC participants to talk to their online "friends" and "followers" about their conversations and interactions with others within a PrLC. Talking publicly about one's own learning is one thing. Drawing attention to other people who expect to conduct business in private is another thing altogether and can completely undermine the process.

The Field of Listening

Both experience and research confirm that technology can *not* replace everything that is done in person. Body language, tone of voice, the way people relate to each other in a physical context, and the use of time are often different in the physical world. The PrLCs are designed to create a live community and a field of listening for people who work together. That goal calls for regular person-to-person meetings in which people develop the capacity to listen fully to and interact with each other. It should be noted, however, that a substantial amount of anecdotal evidence suggests that online communication is enhanced when people have met each other in person as well. So using technology to supplement the PrLCs can be quite effective.

Paying Attention

Evidence suggests that those who multitask online gain some capacities and lose others. In particular, it is possible to become so immersed in the online world that the ability to focus in depth in the real world is weakened. Focusing through our fingers and a camera, while other material flashes by on the screen, is simply different from focusing with the entire body on a physical experience in a real space. One reason for staying with the PrLC is to increase the capacity to sustain our attention and focus when dealing with others in the real world.

→| |← →| |← →| |← →| |←

There is so much to do and to know; so much that is available; so many opinions and possibilities; so many resources.

And so little time.

It is easy to become overwhelmed, and being overwhelmed is of no value to anybody.

So notwithstanding all that can be known and can be done, we strongly recommend that participants take it easy. Choose what you want to focus on. Make sure that it is manageable—neither too cold nor too hot, neither too small nor too large. Then engage to the extent that is just at the edge of your comfort zone. And keep going. After all, irrespective of all the technology that is out there, there is still the phone, and the coffee shop, and the bench in the park.

References

Annenberg Media. *The learning classroom: Theory into practice.* http://www.learner. org/courses/learningclassroom/index.html

Ashby, F. G., Isen, A. M., & Turken, A. U. (1999). A neuropsychological theory of positive affect and its influence on cognition. *Psychological Review, 106*(3), 529–550.

Bandler, R., & Grinder, J. (1975). *The structure of magic: A book about language and therapy.* Palo Alto, CA: Science and Behavior Books.

Bandura, A. (2000). Self-efficacy: The foundation of agency. In W. J. Perrig (Ed.), *Control of human behavior, mental processes, and consciousness* (pp. 17–33). Mahwah, NJ: Lawrence Erlbaum Associates.

Barab, S. A., & Duffy, T. (2000). From practice fields to communities of practice. In D. H. Jonassen & S. M. Land (Eds.), *Theoretical foundations of learning environments* (pp. 25–56). Mahwah, NJ: Lawrence Erlbaum Associates.

Bohm, D. (1996). *Unfolding meaning: A weekend of dialogue with David Bohm.* New York: Routledge.

Briggs Myers, I., & McCaulley, M. (1985). *Manual: A guide to the development and use of the Myers-Briggs Type Indicator.* Palo Alto, CA: Consulting Psychologists Press.

Brighton, C. (2009, February). Embarking on action research. *Educational Leadership, 66*(5), 40–44.

Brothers, L. (1997). *Friday's footprint: How society shapes the human mind.* New York: Oxford University Press.

Caine, G. (2009, Summer). School leader as instructional leader: Finding a path of professional development for educators. *Leadership in Focus: The Journal for Australasian School Leaders, 16.*

Caine, G., & Caine, R. (2001). *The brain, education, and the competitive edge.* Lanham, MD: Scarecrow Press.

Caine, G., & Caine, R. (2008). *Natural learning: The basis for raising and sustaining high standards of real world performance.* Idyllwild, CA: Natural Learning Research Institute.

Caine, G., & Caine, R. (2011). *Seeing education in a new light: Unleashing the power of perceptual change.* New York: Teachers College Press.

Caine, G., Caine R., & Crowell, S. (1999). *Mindshifts* (2nd ed.). Tucson, AZ: Zephyr Press.

Caine, R. (2008). How neuroscience informs our teaching of elementary students. In C. Block, S. Parris, & P. Afflerbach (Eds.), *Comprehension instruction* (2nd ed., pp. 127–141). New York: Guilford Press.

Caine, R., & Caine, G. (1990). Understanding a brain-based approach to learning and teaching. *Educational Leadership,48*(2), 66–70. Alexandria, VA: ASCD.

Caine, R., & G. Caine, (1991). *Making connections: Teaching and the human brain*. Alexandria, VA: ASCD.

Caine, R., & Caine, G. (1994). *Making connections: Teaching and the human brain*. Menlo Park, CA: Addison-Wesley.

Caine, R., & Caine, G. (1997a). *Education on the edge of possibility*. Alexandria, VA: ASCD.

Caine, R., & Caine, G. (1997b). *Unleashing the power of perceptual change: The potential of brain-based teaching*. Alexandria, VA: ASCD.

Caine, R., & Caine, G. (2011). *Making connections: Natural learning, technology and the human brain*. New York: Teachers College Press.

Caine, R., Caine, G., McClintic, C., & Klimek, K. (2008). *The 12 brain/mind learning principles in action* (2nd ed.). Thousand Oaks, CA: Corwin.

California Commission on Teacher Credentialing (July, 1997). *California Standards for the Teaching Profession*. Sacramento: California Department of Education.

Chappius, S., Chappius, J., & Stiggins, R. (2009, February). Supporting teacher learning teams. *Educational Leadership, 66*(5), 56–60.

Claxton, G. (1999). *Hare brain, tortoise mind: How intelligence increases when you think less*. New York: Harper Perennial.

Collay, M., Dunlap, D., Enloe, W., & Gagnon Jr., G. W. (1998). *Learning circles: Creating conditions for professional development*. Thousand Oaks, CA: Corwin.

Combs, A. W. (1999). *Being and becoming*. New York: Springer.

Covey, S. (1998). *The 7 habits of highly effective teens*. New York: Fireside.

Covey, S. R. (2004). *The 7 habits of highly effective people*. New York: Free Press.

Csikszentmihalyi, M. (1990). *Flow: The psychology of optimal experience*. New York: Harper Perennial.

Curwin, R. L., Mendler, A. N., & Mendler, B. D. (2008). *Discipline with dignity: New challenges, new solutions* (3rd ed.). Alexandria, VA: ASCD.

The Dalai Lama. (2001). *An open heart: Practicing compassion in everyday life*. Boston: Little, Brown.

Damasio, A. R. (1999). *The feeling of what happens: Body and emotion in the making of consciousness*. New York: Mariner Books.

Damasio, A. R. (2005). *Descartes' error: Emotion, reason, and the human brain*. New York: Penguin Books.

Darling-Hammond, L., & Richardson, N. (2009, February). Teacher learning: What matters. *Educational Leadership, 66*(5), 46–53.

Davies, L. (2002). Ten ways to foster resiliency in children. Available: http://www.kellybear.com/teacherarticles/TeacherTip25.html

Denkla, M. B. (1999). A theory and model of executive function: A neuropsychological perspective. In G. Lyon & N. Krasnegor, (Eds.), *Attention, memory, and executive function*. Baltimore, MD: Brookes.

Department of Education and Children's Services (DECS). (2004). *Assessing the impact of Phases I and II, Learning to Learn 1999–2004*. South Australia: DECS Publishing.

Donaldson, G. A., Jr. (2009, February). The lessons are in the leading. *Educational Leadership, 66*(5), 14–18.

DuFour, R., Eaker, R., & DuFour, R. (2008). *Revisiting professional learning communities at work: New insights for improving schools*. Bloomington, IN: Solution Tree.

Eliot, T. S. (1971). *The complete poems and plays: 1909–1950*. New York: Harcourt, Brace & World.

Ericsson, K. A., Charness, N., Feltovich, P. J., & Hoffman, R. R. (Eds.). (2006). *Cambridge handbook of expertise and expert performance*. New York: Cambridge University Press.

Ferriter, B. (2009, February). Learning with blogs and wikis. *Educational Leadership, 66*(5), 34–38.

Frankl , V. E. (2006). *Man's search for meaning*. Boston: Beacon Press.

Frost, R. (2002). *Robert Frost's poems*. New York: St. Martin's Paperbacks.

Fuster, J. M. (2003). *Cortex and mind: Unifying cognition*. New York: Oxford University Press.

Gardner, H. (1993). *Frames of mind: The theory of multiple intelligences*. New York: Basic Books.

Gardner, H. (2006). *Multiple intelligences: New horizons in theory and practice*. New York: Basic Books.

Gendlin, E.T. (1982). *Focusing*. New York: Bantam.

Gillham, J. (Ed.). (2000). *The science of optimism and hope: Research essays in honor of Martin E. P. Seligman* (Vol. 2). Radnor, PA: Templeton Foundation Press.

Goleman, D. (2007). *Social intelligence: The new science of human relationships*. New York: Bantam Books.

Gopnik, A., Meltsoff, A. N., & Kuhl, P. (1999). *The scientist in the crib: Minds, brains, and how children learn*. New York: William Morrow.

Gordon, T. (2003). *Teacher effectiveness training: The program proven to help teachers bring out the best in students of all ages*. New York: Three Rivers Press.

Greene, A. J. (2010, July/August). Making connections: The essence of memory is linking one thought to another. *Scientific American Mind*. pp. 22–29.

Greenleaf, R. K., Spears, L. C., & Vaill, P. B. (1998). *The power of servant leadership*. San Francisco: Berrett-Koehler.

Hart, L. (2002). *Human brain and human learning* (3rd ed.). Black Diamond, WA: Books for Educators.

Hartmann, A. C. (2006, September 17). District to try natural learning. *The* [Riverside, CA] *Press Enterprise*.

Hillman, J. (1996). *The soul's code: In search of character and calling*. New York: Warner Books.

Hoff, B. (1982). *The Tao of Pooh, in which The Way is revealed by the Bear of Little Brain*. London: Methuen Children's Books Limited.

Isaacs, W. (1999). *Dialogue and the art of thinking together: A pioneering approach to thinking in business and in life*. New York: Doubleday/Currency.

Jarman, B., & Land, G. (1995). Beyond breakpoint: Possibilities for new community. In K. Gozdz (Ed.), *Community building: Renewing spirit & learning in business* (pp. 21–34). San Francisco: Sterling & Stone.

Kihlstrom, J. F. (2007). *The rediscovery of the unconscious*. University of California, Berkeley. Available: http://socrates.berkeley.edu/~kihlstrm/rediscovery.htm.

Laitsch, D. (2007). Educator community and elementary school performance. *ASCD Research Brief, 5*(2). Available: www.ascd.org/publications/researchbrief/usno2/toc.aspx

Lakoff, G. & Johnson, M. (1999). *Philosophy in the flesh: The embodied mind and its challenge to Western thought*. New York: Basic Books.

Langer, E. (1989). *Mindfulness*. Reading, MA: Addison-Wesley.

Larrivee, B., & Cooper, J. M. (2005). *An educator's guide to teacher reflection*. Stamford, CT: Cengage Learning.

Lave, J., & Wenger, E. (1991). *Situated learning: Legitimate peripheral participation*. New York: Cambridge University Press.

Learning to Learn. (n.d.). Government of South Australia, Department of Education and Children's Services (DECS). Available: http://www.learningtolearn.sa.edu.au

LeCornu, R. (2004). Learning circles: Providing spaces for renewal of both teachers and teacher educators. Australian Teacher Education National Conference Bathurst, NSW, Australia 07/JUL/04 *Making Spaces: Regenerating the Profession*: Proceedings of the 2004 Australian Teacher Education National Conference, p. 141–149.

LeDoux, J. E. (1996). *The emotional brain*. New York: Simon and Schuster.

Leithwood, K., McAdie, P., Bascia, N., & Rodrigue, A. (2006). *Teaching for deep understanding: What every educator should know*. Thousand Oaks, CA: Corwin.

Lindahl, K., & Schnapper, A. (2002). *The sacred art of listening: Forty reflections for cultivating a spiritual practice*. Woodstock, VT: Skylight Paths Publishing.

MacLean, P. D. (1978). A mind of three minds: Educating the triune brain. In J. S. Chall & A. F. Mirsky (Eds.), *Education and the brain: The seventy-seventh yearbook of the national society for the study of education* (pp. 308–342). Chicago: University of Chicago Press.

Murphy, C. U., & Lick, D. W. (2004). *Whole-faculty study groups: Creating professional learning communities that target student learning* (3rd ed.). Thousand Oaks, CA: Corwin.

Nair, K. (1994). *A higher standard of leadership: Lessons from the life of Gandhi*. San Francisco: Berrett-Koehler.

Nieto, S. (2009, February). From surviving to thriving. *Educational Leadership*, 66(5), 8–13.

OECD. (2006). *PISA 2006 results*. Available: http://www.oecd.org/document/2/0,3343,en_32252351_32236191_39718850_1_1_1_1,00.html

Oliver, L. P. (1987). *Study circles: Coming together for personal growth and social change*. Cabin John, MD: Seven Locks Press.

Olsen, B., & Sexton, D. (2009, March). Threat rigidity, school reform, and how teachers view their work inside current education policy contexts. *American Educational Research Journal*, 46(1), 9–44. Available: http://aer.sagepub.com/cgi/content/abstract/46/1/9

Osterman, K. F., & Kottkamp, R. B. (2004). *Reflective practice for educators* (2nd ed.). Thousand Oaks, CA: Corwin.

Perfect, T. J., & Schwartz, B. L. (2002). *Applied metacognition*. New York: Cambridge University Press.

Perry, B. (2000). The neuropsychological impact of childhood trauma. In I. Schulz, S. Carella, & D. O. Brady (Eds.), *Handbook for psychological injuries: Evaluation, treatment and compensable damage*. (Prefinal draft.) Chicago: American Bar Association Publishing.

Pert, C. B. (1997). *Molecules of emotion*. New York: Scribner.

Ravitch, D. (2010). *The death and life of the great American school system: How testing and choice are undermining education*. New York: Basic Books.

Reason, P., & Bradbury, H. (2007). *Handbook of action research* (2nd ed.). London: Sage.

Resnick, L. B. (2010, April). Nested learning systems for the thinking curriculum. *Educational Researcher*, 39, no. 3, pp. 183–197.

Restak, R. (1995). *Brainscapes*. New York: Hyperion.

Rideout, V. J., Foehr, U. G., & Roberts, D. F. (2010). *Generation M2: Media in the lives of 8- to 18-year-olds*. Menlo Park, CA: Kaiser Family Foundation.

Rizzolatti, G., Sinigaglia, C., & Anderson, F. (2008) *Mirrors in the brain: How our minds share actions, emotions, and experience.* New York: Oxford University Press.

Roald, T. (2008) *Cognition in emotion: An investigation through experiences with art.* Consciousness, Literature, and the Arts series. New York: Rodopi.

Sarrio, J. (2009, December 28). High schools chief Jay Steele wants kids grouped by interest. *The Tennessean.*

Schacter, D. (1996). *Searching for memory: The brain, the mind, and the past.* New York: Basic Books.

Schön, D. A. (1990). *Educating the reflective practitioner: Toward a new design for teaching and learning in the professions.* San Francisco: Jossey-Bass.

Schön, D. A. (1995). *The reflective practitioner: How professionals think in action.* Burlington, VT: Ashgate Publishing.

Searle, J. (2010). *Can brain explain mind?* Available http://www.closertotruth.com/video-profile/Can-Brain-Explain-Mind-John-Searle-/158

Seligman, M. E. P. (1991). *Learned optimism.* New York: Pocket Books, Simon & Schuster.

Senge, P. M. (2006). *The fifth discipline: The art and practice of the learning organization.* New York: Doubleday/Currency.

Sousa, D. A. (2008). *How the brain learns mathematics.* Thousand Oaks, CA: Corwin.

Sternberg, R. J. (1985). *Beyond IQ: A triarchic theory of human intelligence.* New York: Cambridge University Press.

Sternberg, R. J. (2008). 5th ed. *Cognitive psychology.* Florence, KY: Wadsworth Publishing

Thompson, E. (2007). *Mind in life: Biology, phenomenology, and the sciences of mind.* Cambridge: Belknap Press.

Toffler, A. (1983). *Previews and premises.* New York: Morrow.

Tuckman, B. (1965, June). Developmental sequence in small groups. *Psychological Bulletin, 63*(6), 384–399. Available: http://findarticles.com/p/articles/mi_qa3954/is_200104/ai_n8943663

University of Oregon Diversity Initiative. Available: http://gladstone.uoregon.edu/~asuomca/diversityinit/definition.html

Van den Heuvel-Panhuizen, M., & Wijers, M. (2005, August). Mathematics standards and curricula in the Netherlands. *ZDM, 37*(4).

Varela, F. J., Thompson, E., & Rosch, E. (1991). *The embodied mind: Cognitive science and human experience.* Cambridge: MIT Press.

Wei, R. C., Andree, A., & Darling-Hammond, L. (2009, February). How nations invest in teachers. *Educational Leadership, 66*(5), 28–33.

Wenger, E., McDermott, R., & Snyder, R. (2002). *Cultivating communities of practice.* Boston: Harvard Business School Publishing.

Wheatley, M. J. (2009). *Turning to one another: Simple conversations to restore hope to the future* (2nd ed.). San Francisco: Berrett-Koehler.

Wheelan, S. A., & Kesselring, J. (2005, July). Link between faculty group development and elementary student performance on standardized tests. *Journal of Educational Research, 98*(6), 323–330.

White Eagle. (1990). *The quiet mind.* Liss, England: White Eagle Publishing Trust.

Index

The letter *f* following a page number denotes a figure.

About the Authors

Geoffrey Caine is a learning consultant, process coach, and writer. He is Codirector of the Caine Learning Center and Executive Director of the Natural Learning Research Institute. Geoffrey has an extensive background in adult education, having been a tenured member of a faculty of law in Australia, Education Services Manager of a national software company, and National Director of the Mind/Brain Network of the American Society of Training and Development. He consults throughout the world on the implementation of natural learning, and works with and gives talks to schools and educational organizations as well as nonprofits, foundations, and businesses. Geoffrey is also an international colleague of one of the world's leading-edge educational reform projects, Learning to Learn in South Australia. Geoffrey can be contacted at Caine Learning Center, Box 1847, Idyllwild, CA 92549. Phone: 951-659-0152. E-mail: Geoffrey@cainelearning.com.

Renate N. Caine is an education consultant, researcher, and writer. She is Codirector of the Caine Learning Center, Director of Research and Professional Development at the Natural Learning Institute, and Professor Emeritus of Education at California State University in San Bernardino (CSUSB). Renate has taught or worked with teachers at every level from kindergarten to university, and her work with schools has been featured on Teacher TV; on the Discovery Channel; on "Wizards of Wisdom," shown on PBS; and elsewhere. She consults throughout the world on the implementation of natural learning, works with schools interested in long-term restructuring, and gives talks to schools and educational organizations. Renate is also an international colleague of one of the world's leading-edge educational reform projects, Learning to Learn in South Australia. Renate can be contacted at Caine Learning Center, Box 1847, Idyllwild, CA 92549. Phone: 951-659-0152. E-mail: Renate@cainelearning.com.

The Caines have written many publications on learning and education. See their website for more information: www.cainelearning. com. Their books include *Making Connections: Teaching and the Human Brain* (1991, ASCD; 1994, Addison Wesley Longman); *Education on the Edge of Possibility* (1997, ASCD); *Unleashing the Power of Perceptual Change: The Potential of Brain-Based Teaching* (1997, ASCD); *Mindshifts* (with Sam Crowell, 1999, Zephyr Press); *The Brain, Education, and the Competitive Edge* (2001, Scarecrow Press); *Natural Learning: The Basis for Raising and Sustaining High Standards of Real World Performance* (2008, Natural Learning Research Institute); *The 12 Brain/Mind Learning Principles in Action* (with Carol McClintic and Karl J. Klimek, 2nd ed., 2008, Corwin); and the forthcoming *Seeing Education in a New Light* (Teachers College Press) and *Natural Learning and Technology: Partners in a New Kind of Education* (Teachers College Press).